Does "freedom of speech" mean freedom to censor?

Apparently, the answer for many in the media today is "yes." In this alarming exposé, Dr. Tim LaHaye unearths the disquieting truth concerning our nation's media: the forces of secular humanism are in control. An ideological monopoly exists—comprised of people who are unsympathetic and often hostile to the traditional values held by most Americans. In the entertainment media, they glorify moral degradation. In the news media, they distort the facts so that they conform to their view of "reality." In the name of *freedom*, they assault us with a barrage of liberal biases, socialistic ideals, and relativistic values—and suppress religious, conservative, and pro-moral expression. What can be done? Dr. LaHaye offers you an effective plan to combat these hidden censors—a plan to defend and exercise our rights as defined by the First Amendment to the U.S. Constitution. With this information put to use, we can *win* the battle for a free media.

The Hidden Censors

Tim LaHaye

Power Books

FLEMING H. REVELL COMPANY
OLD TAPPAN, NEW JERSEY

Scripture quotations are from the *Good News Bible*—Old Testament: Copyright © American Bible Society 1976: New Testament: Copyright © American Bible Society 1966, 1971, 1976.

Library of Congress Cataloging in Publication Data

LaHaye, Tim F.
    The hidden censors

    Bibliography: p.

1. Mass media—United States—Moral and ethical aspects.   2. Mass media—Censorship—United States. I. Title.
P94.L33   1984   001.51′0973   84-1968
ISBN 0-8007-5140-X (pbk.)

Acknowledgements

No author can take full credit for his writings. We are all indebted to other researchers, journalists, teachers, and associates.

In this book I am particularly indebted to Frank York for his able assistance in research and compilation; Linda Matsushima, my excellent secretary, for typing; Michael Jameson for his helpful research; Carol Tubbs for transferring my ideas into meaningful charts and diagrams; and the Fleming H. Revell Company for their courage in publishing this fourth book in my concerted attempt to expose the harmful effects of secular humanist thinkers on our American culture.

Contents

Preface

Before you begin reading this book, I must make something clear: I am a firm believer in the freedom of the press, freedom of speech, and freedom to worship God. I believe that God Almighty blessed our Founding Fathers with the wisdom to write the Declaration of Independence and the Constitution of the United States, with its all-important Bill of Rights.

The First Amendment to the Constitution declares, "Congress shall make no law respecting an establishment of religion, or prohibiting the free exercise thereof; or abridging the freedom of speech, or of the press; or the right of the people peaceably to assemble, and to petition the Government for a redress of grievances."

The *press* mentioned in the First Amendment now includes all forms of communication: film, books, radio, television, newspapers, and magazines. Throughout most of our two-hundred-year history, the free press has been responsible in the exercise of its immense powers.

But during the past fifty years or so, something has happened to the mass media. Gradually, our communications system has been taken over by men and women who for the most part do not share our traditional moral values. It has been seized by people who are much more godless, immoral, or amoral in their outlook than are the American people as a whole. As you will soon learn, we no longer have free media in America. They have been captured by a combination of liberals, socialists, atheists, humanists, and Marxists, who are using the media to change our nation and destroy traditional moral values.

They demand the "freedom" to attack those who do not share their liberal philosophy and "liberated" way of life. With almost complete impunity, they distort, ridicule, and openly criticize religion, patriotism, the free-enterprise system, and conservatism as if they were this nation's principal enemies. When criticized as biased, unfair, or prejudiced, they cry "censorship." In reality, they are the worse censors of all.

Can I prove these charges? Read on. After finishing this book, you will never watch a movie, read a book, view a newscast, or enjoy a television documentary in the same way. Nevertheless, there is hope for recapturing the media from these forces. That hope, however, depends on how you respond to this book.

The Hidden Censors

1

The Power of the Media

The overall way of thinking in the United States has shifted away
from basic Biblical values, and the media share in the responsibility
[for this change].

DR. FRANCIS SCHAEFFER[1]

We must realize that the communications media function much like
the unelected Federal bureaucracy. They are so powerful that they act
as if they were the fourth branch of the government. . . .

DR. FRANCIS SCHAEFFER[2]

Prior to the Revolution, Americans commonly attended church each
week to get caught up on their latest newsworthy events by their
preachers. What a difference in present-day America, where every citizen watches the nightly news or reads a daily newspaper! Those who
report the news often rarely go to church and seem hostile to both the
church and the truth for which it stands.

This may well explain why the official policies and philosophies of
our nation are so out of step with the thinking of the majority of our
people. We have gone from a nation committed to law based on moral
absolutes to a permissive society that has produced violence, family
disruption, and such bizarre consequences of immorality as the herpes
and AIDS epidemics. To this list could be added attacks on the free-
enterprise system by those who prefer the government-guaranteed
life-style of liberal socialism.

In short, America was once officially a God-centered nation. Today
we are man centered. This philosophic transformation has changed
our entire national life, and many of us believe it will destroy our
country. Ironically, polls show that 94 percent of America's people be-

lieve in God, and almost 90 percent give credence to a moral standard based on the Ten Commandments designed by God.

Why has this secular, man-centered thinking process, held by such a small minority, become the official policy of our nation? Many think it is due to the increasing power wielded by the minority who control the media.

The Influence of Modern Media

First, let's define our terms. A *medium* is a means of conveying information; the plural form, *media,* is used when we speak collectively of all forms of communication channels. Therefore media are the vehicles used to reach the minds of people. Those vehicles originated as weekly newspapers, which grew to dailies. Then came magazines, books, radio, movies, wire services, and the most powerful of all—television.

Obviously whoever controls these vehicles of communication will eventually influence patterns of thinking. It is equally obvious that only a handful of people (less than three hundred) can control the philosophy of the material that goes through these media to eventually control the nation.

The media are the conduits used to convey information to the minds of people. For instance the church is a medium used by God to convey His principles for living. If you attend a liberal church, you hear the humanistic philosophy of liberalism. If you attend a Bible-believing church, you hear the truths of God from His Word.

Ever since the advent of newspaper print, an increasing number of antichurch, or in some cases antichristian, individuals have bought newspapers to communicate their liberal humanistic ideas. Then as radio, magazines, and television came into being, these liberal media people were on the ground floor to move right in with authority and experience.

During those years Christians were channeling their energies into carrying out the Great Commission with a worldwide missionary campaign of church building, Bible translation, radio, television, and other ministries (and rightly so). But until recently they have almost totally neglected the powerful media buildup that has burgeoned since

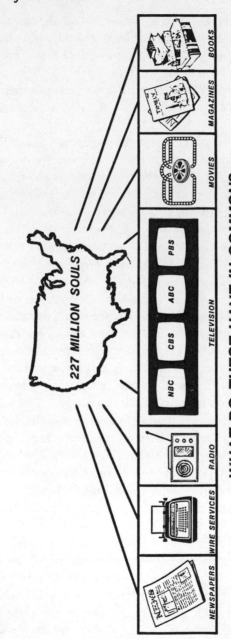

WHAT DO THESE HAVE IN COMMON?

Liberal, Man-centered, A-God or secular, Favor abortion, Accept homosexuality,
Favor big gov't., Soft on Communists, Hard on Conservatives

the turn of the century. Liberal secularists control almost all the major newspapers, national weekly magazines, thousands of radio stations, and the three major networks—even the so-called Public Broadcasting System.

The game plan is really very simple. He who controls the media will ultimately control the government, the schools, and eventually the people.

Have you ever asked yourself why the media, educators, and liberal government bureaucrats think and act rather uniformly, protecting each other and promoting each other? Or why they are all usually out of step with the thinking of the majority of the American people? It is because most of them are secular humanists, while the people still hold to traditional moral values.

The church's power in the media has been limited almost to the walls of the church. The Bible has been largely excluded from our courts, our public schools, and our media. Although the church has powerful influence on its members, *it has little influence on the outside world.* To millions of people in America, the most powerful influences on their thinking processes are the authors of secular books and magazines; editors and journalists of our daily print press; radio disc jockeys and news interpreters; movie producers and screenwriters; and, perhaps heading the list, television program producers, news anchorpersons, and other opinion molders of television.

Unless Christians bestir themselves to move into the media arena, creating Christian television stations in every city throughout the nation and helping to sponsor family television, a television network, and a conservative interpretation of the news to make our ideology competitive with that of liberals who control other media, we will most certainly lose the battle for the minds of our people before the year 2000.

Valiant efforts have been made by Pat Robertson (who established the Christian Broadcasting Network), Jim Bakker (of the PTL Network), and Paul Crouch (of the Trinity Broadcasting Network) to reach American minds through cable television. Added to this number are the other smaller cable networks and popular program producers like Dr. Jerry Falwell, James Kennedy, and many others who are trying to use the media to reach beyond the church and compete with the secular controllers of the media and the battle for the minds of people. Throughout the country, approximately 57 cities now have Christian television stations, out of a possible 241 markets in the nation. Obviously these valiant individuals need to be joined by thousands of others in order to offer an alternative view to the largely antichristian, anticonservative, and sometimes anti-American philosophy of a large percentage of those who control the secular media.

The Power of the Media

It is almost impossible to exaggerate the power of the media. We measure power by its effects on those who use it. Who can deny that television, movies, and secular radio programming are having an oppressively harmful influence on the morals of America? Soap operas depict a hedonistic life-style that dramatically and grippingly shows no respect for traditional moral values, and thus appears as the norm to a nation of viewers. On TV homosexuality achieves a respectability that is questionable biblically and historically. Divorce is rendered commonplace, until it is imitated by 51 percent of those who marry.

Although the media producers, whether print, magazine, or electronic, continually say, "We're only giving the people what they want," they are really fabricating what the media producers and owners believe in and advocate. That amoral, and in some cases immoral, philosophy is gradually destroying our nation's moral fabric. The media's power is seen in its degrading influence not only on the nation's morals, but on everything else: national defense, the environment, nuclear power, economics, and virtually every area of life.

For example, World War II comes to mind. The minute Japan bombed Pearl Harbor, the media launched a national defense campaign and whipped the American patriotic spirit into such a frenzy that we attacked both Japan and Germany at nearly the same time, even though they were in opposite parts of the world. Taking the offensive against the Japanese and Germans was possible because it coincided with the ideology of the media molders, who to this day continually subject us to reliving the atrocities of Hitler and the Japanese through TV, movies, books, and articles. Unfortunately our media molders show very little enthusiasm for whipping up a patriotic spirit regarding the spread of Communism anywhere in the world. We perceive the true colors of the media molders by the way they ignore or play down Communism's atrocities and promote the idealism of Communism, in opposition to the realities of history. The powerful might of the American military was defeated in both Korea and Vietnam by the drum-beating attacks of our liberal media. Vietnam stands as a national disgrace, not because we could not win, but because the media so intimidated our national leaders that they would not let us win. Any tactical movements that threatened to provide victory for our military in Vietnam were vilified by the press, until right was made to look wrong and vice versa.

Media: More Powerful Than Presidents

The media never forgave Congressman Richard Nixon for his part in the conviction of Alger Hiss as a Communist. Therefore, his blundering mistakes of Watergate gave them the opportunity they had long awaited—to publicly humiliate and disgrace him.

President Lyndon Baines Johnson, the fair-haired boy of the media during his first term of office, defied them and showed military strength in Vietnam. Ultimately the liberal Texas politician was so intimidated by media demanding United States withdrawal from Vietnam that he declined to run for a second term.

President Jimmy Carter was swept into office largely due to the hype of the media. Never in my lifetime has a committed liberal politician been made to look more like a conservative in order to get elected. But even a favorable media in 1976 could not cover his liberal appointments, administrative incompetence, and lack of leadership ability.

The biggest disappointment to the liberals of the media during the past fifty years must surely have been the election of Ronald Reagan in 1980. They did everything they could to discredit him, but America's yearning for a strong leader overcame their best efforts. However, they have incessantly criticized and increasingly protested every major decision, and they will do everything in their power to circumvent his valiant attempts to bring America back to traditional moral values, a vibrant economy, and a strong defense policy.

Institution of Power

In my opinion the most powerful institutions in our country today are as follows:

1. Media—press, radio, television
2. Government—federal, state, local
3. Education—43 million schoolchildren and 17 million college students
4. Business—banking institutions and corporations
5. The church—particularly the Bible-believing church
6. Thousands of pressure groups, from the ACLU to NOW, from unions to political organizations

I believe 70 to 80 percent of all these institutions, except the church, are dominated by the liberal philosophy of secular humanism. Its proponents believe that there is no personal God and man is capable of solving his problems independent of God. The American people do not generally accept this philosophy, but it is shared by those few who control these powerful institutions. The media wield great power because their members have the ability to get fellow thinkers into the other institutions of power and keep them there; consequently they inordinately influence American culture.

The thinking of the media does not reflect the thinking of America—it molds it!

Power for Good or Evil

After years of study, I am convinced that the major television networks, many of our most prominent magazines and newspapers, motion-picture studios, book publishing houses, and radio stations have fallen into the hands of men and women who do not share Christian moral values.

The immense power of these unelected leaders of the media, who might be called a media elite, can be used for good or evil. Sadly it serves evil purposes today.

A recent poll shows that most Americans agree with me. An opinion poll, conducted by Yankelovich, Skelly and White, Inc. for *Time* magazine in 1981, found that 60 percent of Americans agreed that "television and other media in this country reflect a permissive and immoral set of values which are bad for the country."[3]

Yet what is being done by the general public to influence the media to change? Apparently very little.

Those who control the media convey to you—the viewer or the reader—*their* view of reality. This view, of course, can be badly distorted by their prejudices, their political ideology, and their feelings of the moment.

During the past thirty years, the mass medium of television has become the most dominant force in American life. Over 98 percent of all homes in America now have television. With the introduction of cable TV, video tape recorders, video disks, video games, and home computers, television is becoming the entertainment center for American families.

As more and more Americans spend time in front of the television, the dangers of mind control become ever greater. *Christianity Today* (May 7, 1982) reported, "Television's power to cultivate an entire view of reality is a challenge that most Christians have not reckoned with. The danger is that while holding the correct set of beliefs about God and His Word, we may be allowing something quite different to shape our minds."[4]

In watching television—the prime medium of communication in our society—we are exposed to what one author has called the "Peeping Tom" reality.

We need to be aware of six general characteristics of television if we are to intelligently evaluate what we are seeing:

1. Television ignores the reality of God and His work in our world. But it does more than *ignore* the reality of God. In recent years, Christianity has been aggressively attacked by those who control television.

2. The population on TV differs drastically from the real population in America. There is a marked bias in the ages of the characters presented. People under twenty and over sixty are more rare than in the general population. This age bias is rooted in the belief of advertisers that their best potential customers are within the eighteen to forty-nine age group.

3. While God is either ignored or attacked on television, Satan and sin are dealt with in lurid detail. Such obvious sins as adultery, fornication, incest, and drunkenness are glorified—made to seem fun, noble, free. A make-it-up-as-you-go morality is subtly advocated.[5]

4. Problem solving is simplified on TV. Every difficulty, no matter how overwhelming, is usually resolved in 30-, 60- or 120-minute segments.

5. In watching a sports event, newscast, or documentary, we are led to believe we have actually seen an event, when in reality we have only seen *portions* of an event from the reporter's perspective.

    As *Christianity Today* noted, "This moral confusion weakens the conviction that any behavior can be seriously and profoundly wrong. The Christian has more than a moral code. . . . The Christian ought to be angered at serious sin. But as one writer, Stephen Clark, has noted, 'Christians are too often angry about that which offends them and complacent about that which offends God. . .' "[6]

6. Television presents images in such a way as to communicate to the viewer that this life is all there is; there's no afterlife, so get all you can while you're here.

These same criticisms of television can also be applied to newspapers, magazines, film, and radio.

In his book *What Is Secular Humanism?* Dr. James Hitchcock, professor of history at Saint Louis University, has devoted a chapter to the discussion of how the media became corrupted and blatantly antichristian in their content.

The media, says Hitchcock, has undergone a profound moral revolution since the 1960s. ". . . The mass media began to change around

1965, with the most dramatic changes occurring during the 1970s. The changes were related to the pervasive prosperity of the period, and to the cult of self-worship which this produced."[7]

The Vietnam War, the drug culture, and antiestablishment rock music brought a breakdown in moral values among the youth. Those controlling the mass media quickly realized they could capitalize on this growing disenchanted subculture in our traditionally moral society. Movies, books, magazines began catering to this newly created class within our society.

As this revolution took place people who still clung to traditional moral values simply sat back and did nothing to stop the revolution in the media. As Hitchcock clarifies, ". . . If the revolution in the media had been supported solely by self-conscious moral rebels, its scope would have been far narrower. The manipulators of the media also suspected, correctly as it turned out, that many people who professed traditional values would nonetheless accept the new iconoclasm simply as entertainment, without examining too closely the values behind it."[8]

We can trace the results of this moral revolution most clearly in films and on television. In the mid-sixties, filmmakers began very carefully to display women nude from the back or totally nude from a distance. Year after year, this assault on traditional morality became bolder and bolder. Today, an R-rated movie is usually filled with scenes of full frontal nudity, cursing, and graphic, bloody violence.

Over the years even traditional moralists have been desensitized to nudity, cursing, and violence. We have been gradually conditioned to accept behavior that would have shocked us only a few years ago.

The modern mass media have the power to alter our senses of reality—to confuse us—and often we fail to realize how we have been changed.

The Media Push Their Own Ideology

The media have the power to confer respectability on men and ideas. Dr. Hitchcock observes, "To be noticed by a mass audience is almost a kind of canonization. No matter how seemingly 'neutral' the treatment, when certain ideas are given time and space in the media, they acquire a respectability that increases with frequency. . . . There is a deep hypocrisy in the media's pious claims that they merely reflect reality and do not shape it. In fact, the power of celebrity is used deliberately and selectively in order to effect changes in values."[9]

The media—through ridicule and satire—have the power to destroy traditional value systems. Perhaps no one has tried to do more damage to traditional Judeo-Christian morality in recent years than TV producer Norman Lear. Producer of "All in the Family," "Maude," "Mary Hartman, Mary Hartman," "Different Strokes," and other programs, Lear has inflicted audiences with seemingly mindless comedy fare for over a decade. Yet his comedies are in actuality deadly serious in their content.

In "All in the Family," for example, Archie Bunker was supposed to typify the average American—a stupid, bigoted, moralistic, intolerant man, unwilling to listen to the "rational" and "humane" arguments of his liberal daughter and son-in-law.

Norman Lear's comedies are deliberately being used as vehicles for his brand of liberal propaganda. Lear even hired a woman named Virginia Carter, described by *Esquire* magazine as "a fervent feminist and a passionate liberal," to work her favorite leftist philosophies into each show. As Ms. Carter put it, "I consider it a duty to serve as an advocate. To waste that valuable air space I'd have to be a crazy lady."[10]

Norman Lear is a liberal activist who has been a longtime supporter of the American Civil Liberties Union, National Organization for Women, the feminist movement, and the California Citizens Action Group. More recently he has become known for his founding of People for the American Way—an aggressive, antichristian group working to destroy the Moral Majority and other groups seeking to exercise religious freedom in America.

In describing the purpose of People for the American Way, Norman Lear alleges that he is just trying to protect "the nature of our pluralistic society." His group purposes "to help people work and enjoy their liberties by using them. The country needs to know what people feel about the issues and we want to motivate Americans to express themselves for a healthier society."[11]

Conservative columnist John Lofton identified the true intent of this liberal rhetoric about free speech when he wrote, ". . . The disagreements between P.A.W. and the religious New Right are about something far more tangible than the right of free expression or free thought. This is a battle about whose thoughts or expressions will prevail. This is a fight about whether it should be legal to kill innocent unborn children; whether those kids who want to should be allowed to pray in the public schools; whether children should be forcibly bused to schools not of their choosing; whether parents should have any say about their kids' sex education."[12]

I am firmly convinced that men like Norman Lear are not truly concerned about freedom of expression and rational discussion of issues by opposing groups. They are propagandists for the philosophy of humanism—a godless philosophy that promotes the false notion that man is the center of all things and that all morality is what man says it is—that if it feels good, he should do it.

In discussing Norman Lear and his character Archie Bunker, Dr. Hitchcock noted, "Lear was praised for going beyond mere entertainment to give audiences 'thoughtful' comedies. But his programs were mainly devices for disseminating his own ideology. . . . Since Archie believed in God, country, family and traditional sexual morality, those beliefs were tarred. . . . Obviously, no humane, thoughtful person could hold such beliefs. For contrast, Lear's programs also presented people who dissented from such values, models of rational humaneness."[13]

Lear, together with A. Jerrold Perenchio, purchased the Avco-Embassy movie studio several years ago for $25 million. You can be sure that his liberal/humanist propaganda will continue to pour out through his movies.

Donald Wildmon Takes a Stand Against Immorality on TV

Methodist minister Donald Wildmon of Tupelo, Mississippi, has probably done more than anyone else in America in recent years to take a strong, godly stand against the pervasive immorality and antichristian tone of television today.

His monthly newspaper, the *NFD Informer,* now has a circulation of over 200,000 and he is making a positive impact on television by letting moral Americans know what is being done to them in the name of entertainment.

In Wildmon's opinion, the ultimate power of television is its power to teach—to transmit values. As Wildmon wrote in the April, 1982, issue of *Religious Broadcasting,*

> All television is educational. That being true, what is it teaching?
> It is teaching that adultery is an acceptable and approved lifestyle.
> It is teaching that violence is a legitimate way to achieve one's goals or to resolve conflict. It is teaching that profanity is the language of the respectable. But these are only surface messages. The real message is deeper.
> It is teaching that hardly anyone goes to church, that very few people in our society are Christian or live by Christian principles. How? By simply censoring out Christian characters, Christian values, and Christian culture from the programs. It is teaching that people who claim to be Christians are hypocrites, cheats, liars or the like. It does that by characterization.[14]

The Power of Imitation, Modeling, and Provoking Violence Through TV

The awesome power of the media is also evident in its ability to provoke imitations of the behavior depicted on the screen or in the press.

In January of 1983, David P. Phillips, a professor of sociology at the University of California in San Diego, released his study on the response of television viewers to seven suicide reports between 1972 and 1976. He correlated the day-to-day suicide rates between 1972 and 1976, trying to determine if suicides increased after a major suicide report.

Phillips stated, "For a very brief period of time, U.S. suicides increase significantly just after the appearance of a non-fictional suicide story carried by the network evening news." He reported that following each suicide story, the increase was about twenty-eight deaths per story nationwide in the week following. He based his study on suicide figures provided by the National Center of Health Statistics.

Phillips has also explored what is called "imitative suicide." Earlier research has shown that fatal, single-car crashes also increase after major news stories on suicides and that people will kill themselves after viewing a soap-opera character who commits suicide on the show. Phillips observed, "Taken together, all of these findings support the hypothesis that publicized suicides trigger imitative behavior, sometimes this behavior is overt (in the form of an explicit suicide) and sometimes covert (in the form of automobile or airplane accidents)."

What causes people to imitate the behavior they see on TV? Phillips doesn't really know. "What is it that makes somebody want to buy something that's advertised on television when a prestigious or impressive individual is shown using it? Who knows why that is? ... I think what's going on in advertising is an artificial form of what's going on in the stuff I'm studying, which is, you might say, national advertising."[15]

There are many examples of the media serving as a catalyst for either antisocial or self-destructive behavior. For example, since the movie *The Deer Hunter* began playing in theaters in 1979, at least twenty-five viewers have reenacted the Russian roulette scene in the movie and have blown their brains out. The latest reported victim is a seventeen-year-old from Denver.

Ted Turner, owner of Cable News Network and WTBS in Atlanta, is livid about the sex and violence on TV and in our movies. He was particularly disturbed about *The Deer Hunter*. "... There was not one single documented example anywhere in Vietnam where the Vietnamese forced Americans to blow their brains out," said Turner. "That was just dreamed up. As if the war wasn't bad enough!"[16]

In San Diego a high-school honor student watched an ABC movie on the life of Lizzie Borden, the notorious ax murderer of the 1890s. Shortly after that he hacked his mother, father, and sister to death. His surviving brother must live the rest of his life as a quadriplegic.[17]

Then, of course, there's John Hinckley, Jr., the young man who attempted to murder President Reagan in 1981. Hinckley had become obsessed with teenage actress Jodi Foster after watching the movie *Taxi.* In this movie, Robert de Niro played the role of a psychopath who became a vigilante and killed people to "protect" Jodi Foster. Hinckley was apparently inspired to kill President Reagan after watching the film.

It is my conviction that moviemakers, producers of TV programming, and far too many journalists are provoking sexual immorality and violence in our society by continuing to graphically portray sex and violence in the media. Those who control the media act irresponsibly in the exercise of their right of free speech. They apparently have no conception of the difference between *liberty* and *license.* The media moguls wield immense power, yet this power is being used to destroy our culture, concepts of right and wrong, and family ties.

Somehow our masters of the media who demand the freedom to express their ideas must be made to realize that they must bear the responsibility of the abuse of freedom. Freedom without responsibility always leads to chaos. The ultimate end of unrestrained freedom in media will be a society destroyed by anarchy.

Children and Televised Violence

According to the National Coalition on Television Violence, the prime-time programs now average eight violent acts per hour. This is 400 percent higher than two Canadian networks and nine times more violent than PBS-produced programming.

The coalition also released findings in January of 1983 that cable and subscription (pay) television are even more violent than regular network programming. According to this new study, pay cable TV is three times more violent than network programming.

After monitoring two months of summer and fall prime-time programs on Home Box Office, Showtime, and the Movie Channel, the coalition discovered ten times more violence on pay cable channels than Public Broadcasting Service programs.[18]

In a recently released ten-year update on the surgeon general's report on TV violence, a panel of experts agree that a definite cause-and-effect relationship exists between TV violence and real-life aggression.

According to Thomas Radecki, chairman of the National Coalition on Television Violence and psychiatry professor at Southern Illinois University, "Violence in our society has increased 300% to 500% since 1957, when television first became markedly more violent. I expect this violence to continue to grow as HBO, Hollywood movies, and network TV continue their emphasis on violent entertainment. Unless we act now, I fear that the future of American democracy may soon be at stake."[19]

Radecki points out that over 700 scientific studies show that entertainment violence causes 25 percent to 50 percent of everyday family anger and aggression.

The highly publicized Tylenol poisonings in Chicago are a case in point. Some madman laced the most popular painkiller of our day with cyanide poison, resulting in three deaths. Within hours the homes of Americans were bombarded with the news; within days this bizarre and fiendish crime occurred in Denver, Los Angeles, Oregon, and other places. Who says the media aren't powerful?

Children, of course, are particularly vulnerable to entertainment violence. From the age of six to eighteen, the average child spends 16,000 hours watching television, compared to only 12,000 hours in school. A typical child only spends more time sleeping than he does watching TV.

According to a 1982 Nielsen Report on television, the average family keeps the TV on forty-nine and a half hours a week. The typical teenager graduating from high school will have watched the equivalent of ten years of forty-hour weeks. He will have viewed approximately 150,000 violent episodes and probably as many as 25,000 killings.[20]

Perhaps the most disturbing thing about television violence is that the early-morning cartoons your children watch are more violent than most prime-time programs. Eugene Methvin writes, ". . . The Saturday-morning 'kid vid' ghetto is the most violent time on TV. It bathes the prime audience of youngsters from 3 to 13 years old with 25 violent acts per hour, much of it in a poisonous brew of violent programs and aggressive commercials . . ."[21]

The Television Commission of the National PTA reported that, "Cartoon violence, often more subtle because it is masked by amusing and attractive illustration, was cited often as a contributor to the effect of distortion, since death and injury are utterly unreal."[22]

Are cartoons harmless? A cartoon killed six-year-old Jeremy Nezworski. In the October 5, 1982, issue of *Family Circle,* his mother tells the story of his tragic death.[23]

Jeremy, six, and his four-year-old brother, Brad, had been watching a morning cartoon show about a dog who chases ghosts. In the cartoon, there had been a figure hanging on a hook, with a white hood over its head. Jeremy thought he would play a game, so he went upstairs with Brad, deciding to imitate what he had seen on the cartoon. Jeremy pulled out a pillowcase and found a shoelace in a skate.

Brad sat on the floor, watching, as Jeremy tied the lace around the closet doorknob, climbed onto the end of a shelf, and put the pillowcase over his head. He wound the string five times around his neck and tied it in a double knot. He then stepped off the shelf and slowly suffocated to death as his brother Brad looked on. Too young to really comprehend what was happening, Brad went downstairs to tell his mother that he thought something was wrong.

Jeremy Nezworski died a few days later—an unwitting victim of a cartoon.

Is anything being done to put an end to the incessant sex and violence on television? Several conservative or Christian organizations are doing what they can to put pressure on the networks to act more responsibly. Naturally the censors who control the media call it "censorship." One such organization is the Clean Up TV campaign, headed by John Hurt. Says Hurt, "We're not trying to take any shows off the air. And we're not trying to force our moral judgments on anybody else. What we're really trying to do is get them to clean up the act some—I mean explicit scenes, adultery, sexual perversion, incest. We are asking every morally decent person to speak up and let his position be known."[24]

Don Wildmon, founder of the Coalition for Better Television, became disturbed over sex and violence on TV back in 1977. He resigned his pastorate at the Southaven First United Church and began organizing families and friends to monitor TV programs and record the instances of sex and violence in each program. What started as a modest effort has since grown into a nationwide coalition of Christian and conservative groups working together to clean up television. Today over 2,000 groups are working with Wildmon, who has more than 4,000 trained monitors watching and reporting on television programming.

As Wildmon tells it, "We believe in freedom. We look at it this way: the networks have a right to spend their money any way they want to. . . . And the consumer has a right to spend his money the way he wants to."[25]

Wildmon and the coalition have organized a nationwide boycott and letter-writing campaign directed against the sponsors of programs that consistently promote sexual immorality and violent behavior or that directly attack and ridicule Christianity.

Although the media moguls won't admit it, they have felt enormous pressure by advertisers to clean up their act. Some programs have improved, while others go as far as the law and the advertisers will let them.

The Hidden Censors Give Us Their Reality

The media monopolists have the power not only to provoke antisocial and self-destructive behavior in those who are exposed to their messages but to define what is "real" and what is not "real."

Dr. Hitchcock explains it this way: "What is presented in the media, and the way in which it is presented, is for many people the equivalent of what is real. By determining what ideas will be discussed in public, the media determine which ideas are to be considered respectable, rational and true. Those excluded from discussion, or treated only in a negative way, are conversely defined as disreputable, irrational and false."[26]

If an individual or particular view of life (like Christianity) is denied access to the mass media, the individual or idea will have little chance of gaining a fair hearing with the public. How can Americans make intelligent choices among competing ideas if one side is consistently refused a hearing?

The liberal/humanist bias of the mass media, in effect, declares as "nonexistent" or "irrelevant" any view other than its own. Whenever it is reluctantly forced to allow an opposing viewpoint, it invariably distorts the meaning of the opposition's view. For instance, an ABC "Nightline" program hosted by Ted Koppel considered the subject of herpes, the incurable venereal disease that has already infected 20 million Americans. Evangelist James Robison was allowed five minutes on the thirty-minute show to present the biblical viewpoint, which he did cogently, pointing out that this epidemic, which infects at least 500 new fornicators each year, is the result of God's judgment on sin. Koppel then looked into the camera and remarked, "Now for a less judgmental point of view"—a typical TV put-down of the biblical viewpoint.

1984

Unfortunately, our modern mass communications system functions as in the world depicted by ex-Communist George Orwell in his book *1984*. This classic attack on all totalitarian governments, tells the story of Winston Smith, a worker at the so-called Ministry of Truth. It was Smith's job to rewrite history, making it conform to the current Party Line. The original documents, whether newspaper articles, films, or political cartoons, were tossed down the "memory hole," where they were burned up. In effect, "truth" became whatever the ruling dictatorship said it was. And "truth" could change daily, depending upon current Party doctrine.

When Smith was jailed as a suspected traitor to the Party, his interrogator, O'Brien, gave Smith a lecture on the Party's view of reality and truth. Read carefully what O'Brien says to Smith. It will give you an understanding of the thinking of many contemporary media personalities.

> "Only the disciplined mind can see reality, Winston," warned O'Brien. "You believe that reality is something objective, external, existing in its own right. You also believe that the nature of reality is self-evident. When you delude yourself into thinking that you see something, you assume that everyone else sees the same thing as you.
>
> "But I tell you, Winston, that reality is not external. Reality exists in the human mind, and nowhere else. Not in the individual mind, which can make mistakes, and in any case soon perishes; only in the mind of the Party, which is collective and immortal. *Whatever the Party holds to be truth is truth. It is impossible to see reality except by looking through the eyes of the Party."* [Emphasis added.][27]

Today our mass communications media are under the control of men and women who reflect liberal, humanistic thinking patterns. They only want us to see the world through *their* eyes, because they feel they have been given the "right" to determine "truth" for each of us. With few exceptions, whatever we read in our magazines, books, and newspapers, see on television, or hear on the radio has been filtered through the liberal/humanist biases of these hidden censors of the media. Today, whatever the media elite holds to be truth is truth. It is impossible to see reality except by looking through the eyes of the media elite—or so they think.

Just who are these hidden censors? Where do they *really* stand on political, spiritual, and moral issues?

The Hidden Censors
of the Media

We Americans are probably the most information-oriented people in the world. It has been estimated that 30 million newspapers are sold each morning and another 27 million in the evening. On Sundays we purchase something like 43 million papers for leisurely afternoon reading. Some researchers have estimated that if one combined the circulations of newspapers and magazines purchased weekly in America, the total would approximate 380.4 million.[1]

A recent survey also pointed out that 66 percent of the population receives its primary source of news through television. Actually, people watch television for three main reasons: news, sports, and religious programming. In view of our insatiable appetite for news, it is little wonder that a program like "60 Minutes" is often the highest rated show on television.[2]

As a nation we are literally saturated with various forms of communication: radio, TV, computers, books, magazines, newspapers. Yet, in the midst of this virtual deluge of information, can we really believe what we are being told about the world around us?

In 1981, shortly after the infamous Janet Cooke/Pulitzer Prize fraud at the *Washington Post,* a nationwide Gallup Poll was conducted to test the public's confidence in the news media as a whole. Pollsters discovered that 61 percent believed "very little" or "only some" of the news. Journalists also rated last in a ranking based on ethical standards and honesty. Top ranking went to the clergy, 71 percent; doctors, 58 percent; police, 52 percent; and journalists, 38 percent.[3]

Since that poll was conducted, public confidence in the news media has sagged even further. As *U.S. News & World Report* observed, "America's press, which often views itself as a knight on a white horse, is finding that the public sees its once shining armor has badly tarnished."[4]

According to the article, a Harris Survey conducted in 1981 verified that the credibility of the press and electronic media had plummeted to its lowest point ever. Only 24 percent of the people surveyed reflected a great deal of confidence in television news. The figure for the press was only 16 percent. In 1973, when a similar poll was taken, 41 percent of the people trusted television news, and 30 percent expressed confidence in the print media.

In a speech to fellow publishers, James K. Batten, president of Knight-Ridder Newspapers, remarked, "The truth is, a lot of the American public don't much like us or trust us. They think we're too big for our britches."[5]

Jean Otto, an editor at the *Milwaukee Journal,* puts it this way: "The press suffers from arrogance. . . . Sometimes people in the press act as if they are doing their jobs for each other and maybe God, and nobody else ought to get in the way."[6] The trouble with this statement is that an inordinate number in the media don't believe in God, and a significant percentage use their elitist position of power to propagate their anti-God, anti-moral and often anti-American philosophy.

Researchers at Michigan State University recently conducted a survey for the American Society of Newspaper Editors on the attitudes of the press. They found that many reporters were deeply cynical about the public's intelligence. "In some news rooms," said the researchers, "the public-be-damned attitude reached siege mentality."[7]

One possible sign of the public's increasing distrust of the news media is reflected in the huge libel settlements being granted by jurors to individuals who have been defamed by the media. Just in the past few years, juries have awarded defendants millions of dollars in damages: $4.5 million against the *San Francisco Examiner;* $26 million against *Penthouse* magazine; $9.2 million against the *Alton Telegraph,* in Illinois; and $1.6 million against the *National Inquirer.* "The verdicts signify fury," says Bruce Sanford, a Washington press lawyer. "Punishing awards may be the public's way of saying that there are not satisfactory vehicles in the country for registering displeasure with the news media."[8]

According to the Libel Defense Resource Center, "Since 1980 press defendants have lost forty-two of forty-seven libel cases that reached juries. In more than half the cases, awards were over $100,000."[9]

That the media have become increasingly arrogant and irresponsible in the use of their immense powers will become obvious throughout the remainder of this book. As you will see, the public distrust of the media is well founded.

Freedom of the Press

The great Russian author Aleksandr Solzhenitsyn clearly perceived the corruption of the American mass media. In his commencement address at Harvard University in 1978, Solzhenitsyn declared:

> Hastiness and superficiality are the psychic diseases of the twentieth century and more than anywhere else this disease is reflected in the press. In-depth analysis of a problem is anathema to the press. It stops at sensational formulas. . . .
>
> Enormous freedom exists for the press—but not for the readership, because newspapers mostly give stress and emphasis to those opinions which do not too sharply contradict their own, or the general trend.
>
> Without any censorship, fashionable trends of thought and ideas in the West are carefully separated from those which are not fashionable; nothing is forbidden, but what is not fashionable will hardly ever find its way into periodicals or books or be heard in the colleges.[10]

The press, Solzhenitsyn contends, censors simply by ignoring those ideas or individuals not fitting the current political or social philosophy of those controlling the mass media.

As Franky Schaeffer has pointed out so well, "In essence, the major news organizations of the United States do not represent what can be called a free press. A free press requires the presence of organizations which compete not merely to see whether CBS, NBC, or ABC can predict the outcome of an election thirty seconds ahead of its sisters, *but organizations which present distinctly and substantially different points of view.*"[11]

I find it very encouraging that some members of the press are finally admitting that the news media has been irresponsible in the exercise of its powers.

One such journalist is Michael J. O'Neill, former editor of the *New York News*. In May of 1982, O'Neill delivered what I consider candid warning to his fellow journalists at a meeting of the American Society of Newspaper Editors. He pointed out that members of the media—whether print or electronic—have become so enthralled with "investigative" reporting and "adversary" journalism that they have actually threatened to upset the democratic processes in our country.

According to O'Neill, "The extraordinary powers of the media, most convincingly displayed by network television and the national press, have been mobilized to influence major public issues and national elections, to help diffuse the authority of Congress and to disassemble the political parties—even to make presidents or to break them. Indeed, the media now weigh so heavily on the scales of power that some political scientists claim we are upsetting the historic checks and balances invented by our forefathers."

O'Neill warns that members of the media no longer just cover the news—they *create* it; they no longer look at government with healthy skepticism—they view government as an *enemy* to be destroyed.

"No longer do we submit, automatically, to the rigors of old-fashioned impartiality," he concedes. "Now, not always but too often, we surrender to the impulse of advocacy, in the name of reform but forgetful of balance, fairness and—if it isn't too unfashionable to say so—what is good for the country."

Television, especially, bypasses the traditional democratic processes by establishing a direct link between the president and the people—instead of the people dealing with their duly elected representatives in Congress.

"The President no longer has much leverage over the members of Congress, even those in his own party," observes O'Neill. "Congress itself is in a disheveled state with power so diluted that neither floor leaders nor committee chairmen are able to act with the authority, for example, of a Sam Rayburn."

Michael J. O'Neill also notes that two phenomena have brought about chaos in government: "... the press's harshly adversarial posture toward government and its infatuation with investigative reporting. These attitudes, which have always lurked in the psyche of American journalists, were enormously intensified by Vietnam, Watergate and the general attack on authority in the 1960s and 1970s. Both news coverage and the conduct of government have been duly affected—but not improved."

What does O'Neill suggest as a solution to this problem with the media? He feels that members of the media should:

1. Be more positive and more sensitive to the rights and feelings of individuals—public officials and private citizens.
2. Journalists should be less arrogant, recognizing their own shortcomings. They have no corner on "truth."
3. Journalists should make peace with the government. "Our assignment is to report and explain issues, not decide them."
4. Journalists need to have a value system that prevents them from needlessly hurting public figures.
5. Journalists must resist "the pseudo event, the phoney charges, the staged protest, the packaged candidate, the prime-time announcement...."[12]

While I can applaud Michael O'Neill's willingness to speak the truth about the bias and corruptive power of the media, I am also aware that the members of the press are extremely resistant to anything that would restrict their "right to know" and their "right to tell." I do not believe that the press—as a whole—is responsible enough at this point to engage in any kind of effective self-regulation.

I find it intriguing that, while the press can lobby and push for consumer legislation to protect Americans from business fraud, it goes into hysterics if someone suggests that we might need some government legislation requiring "truth in reporting." In essence, members of the media have set themselves up as a power center in America—totally unrestrained by either government or the people—operating with impunity and arrogance, telling us how we should live and think. Perhaps we *do* need some kind of truth-in-reporting law or at least a media review board.

Interpretative Reporting

For a number of years, young, eager journalists were taught the five *W*s of journalism in college: *Who, what, where, when,* and *why.* These were the basic facts utilized in the reporting process. They were also admonished to be *objective,* reporting the news but being careful to present *both* sides of an issue. They were not to take sides, but were to try—as much as possible—to be fair in the presenting of opposing viewpoints, even viewpoints they personally detested.

As journalists they were not to set themselves up as judges of right and wrong. As members of the free press it was their responsibility to present various sides of controversial issues and then let the American people make up their own minds.

If they were caught editorializing in their news reports, those portions would quickly be blue penciled by the editor. Editorializing belonged *only* on the editorial page.

In the 1924 edition of *Editorial Writing: Ethics, Policy, Practice,* the dean of the School of Journalism at Syracuse University, Dr. Lyle Spencer, wrote, "One must decry the ambition of any editor to mold the opinion of his readers according to his standards. Molding opinion means shaping it—warping often—according to the ideals or opinions of a single person or group of individuals."[13]

Spencer advocated the traditional viewpoint that except for the editorial page, the newspaper was to report straight facts and leave the conclusions up to the readers. "As far as possible," cautioned Spencer, "personal opinion and editorial bias should be excluded from the news columns. . . . The news columns are the possession of the readers. Presentation of unbiased news there, all the news, is their demand and right." *Interpretation* of the news, he insisted, "is the prime function of the editorial." Reporters were free to interpret from their own viewpoints as much as they wished—but only on the editorial page.[14]

Unfortunately, times changed. In 1932 a young journalist named Curtis D. MacDougall published a college textbook, *Reporting for Beginners.* In 1938 the text was revised and renamed *Interpretative Reporting.* This book has been required reading for journalism students at literally hundreds of colleges for nearly half a century.

The writings of Dr. Curtis MacDougall contributed significantly to the demise of "objective" reporting and the rise of "interpretative" reporting.

The reporter, said MacDougall, must be well versed in every field of human endeavor so he can do more than just present facts to his reader. The reporter must select the facts he wants to present and then interpret them according to his own personal feelings and impressions. According to MacDougall, "The interpreter of the news must see reasons where ordinary individuals observe only overt happenings.... Doing his best, he will err constantly; scientific method is nothing but being as approximately correct as possible. His mistakes, however, will be honest ones of an expert and not the blunders of an ignoramus."[15]

Notice what MacDougall has implied. The reporter is not an "ordinary" person. He is an "expert" who must explain to "ordinary" people what "really" happened in a news event. Of course, he will constantly be wrong, but at least he is not an ignoramus or an "ordinary" person.

MacDougall quotes Marquis W. Childs: "The interpretive reporter expands the horizon of the news. He explains, he amplifies, he clarifies.... One of the most important tasks of the interpretive reporter is to expand the peripheries of the news ... it is the special duty of the interpretive reporter to go behind the handout and the press conference."[16]

What Curtis MacDougall has successfully done with his theory of interpretative reporting is to destroy the concept of objectivity in reporting the news. He has taken interpretation—which rightfully belongs on the editorial page—and has applied it to the reporting of *all* news.

In effect, this has given journalists the right to insinuate their opinions, prejudices, and feelings into every story. And they can justify writing blatantly biased news reports under the guise of "interpretative" reporting.

The abuse of so-called interpretative reporting was so rampant during the 1960 presidential election that four independent studies of bias in the news were conducted by news agencies or press-related organizations.

Former *San Diego Union* editor Richard Pourade completed one of these studies a year after the election. In his study, he investigated the bias in hundreds of Associated Press and United Press International news reports. In his summary Pourade wrote, "Wire service reporters set themselves up as a final judge of crowds, reactions, sincerity of statement, pertinency of the statements politically and ideologically, and passed judgments on the merits of the various proposals. Too often, what the candidate had to say was buried beneath how the reporter personally evaluated it in the context of the whole campaign, and what he thought was the crowd's reaction to it."[17]

That, of course, is the terrible legacy left by Curtis MacDougall's "interpretative" reporting. The end result of his kind of journalism is to set up every reporter as a little philosopher-king who arrogates to himself the right to tell his readers—or viewers—his interpretation of the events in the news. No longer do we get facts presented by an impartial reporter; we receive news filtered through his prejudices, his ignorance, his emotions, and his political commitment—which almost always represents liberal/humanist philosophy.

Who is this journalist whose textbook has been used by thousands of journalism students during the past fifty years? Curtis D. MacDougall was born in Fond du Lac, Wisconsin, in 1903. He graduated from Ripon College with a B.A. in 1923, received an M.S. from Northwestern University in 1926 and a Ph.D. at the University of Wisconsin in 1933. During his career in journalism, he worked as a staff correspondent for the Chicago bureau of United Press, taught journalism at Lehigh University, worked for the *Saint Louis Star-Times*, and served as editor of the *Evanston* (Illinois) *Daily News-Index* from 1934 through 1937. In 1942 he was an editorial writer for the *Chicago Sun*. He was a professor of journalism at Northwestern University from 1942 to 1973.[18]

Dr. MacDougall has enjoyed a distinguished career in journalism, but his political activities have showed a distinctly liberal bent. In 1948 he ran for the United States Senate on the Progressive Party ticket in Illinois. MacDougall also served from 1946 to 1956 as an advisor on academic freedom with the left-leaning American Civil Liberties Union, which, in my opinion, has done much to destroy the traditional moral and religious values of America.

As a professor of journalism at a prestigious university, Curtis MacDougall has had a profound influence on American journalism. I be-

lieve his "interpretative" reporting philosophy has given carte blanche
to liberal/humanist reporters to use their personal opinions in describing the news. He is only one of many journalism professors in the
3,000 colleges and universities of America who see in their students the
future change agents of the media.

The Liberal/Humanist Bias and the Media Elite

During 1979 and 1980, two sociologists, S. Robert Lichter and Stanley Rothman, conducted a study on *elites* in America, under the authority of the Research Institute on International Change at Columbia
University. What these two men discovered about our supposedly free
press is shocking, but it simply confirms what I have felt about the
media for many years.

In their study, they conducted hour-long interviews with 240 journalists and broadcasters at the most influential media outlets: *New
York Times, Washington Post, Wall Street Journal, Time, Newsweek,
U.S. News & World Report,* CBS, NBC, ABC, PBS, and others. They
selected their interviewees at random from among reporters, columnists, department heads, bureau chiefs, editors, producers, film editors,
anchormen, and others. In addition, they interviewed business leaders
at seven *Fortune 500* companies, "ranging from a multinational oil
company to a nationwide retail chain." Again the interviewees were
chosen at random to assure the accuracy of the study.

Their findings make fascinating reading. Lichter and Rothman observe, "The influence of the press is based not only on money or political power but on the information and ideas they transmit to other social leaders, as well as to the general public. Even those who question
the media's power to persuade grant their ability to help set the agenda
for discussions about social policy." [19]

Here is what Lichter and Rothman discovered about the men and
women who control our so-called free press.

The media elite is composed mainly of white males in their thirties
and forties. Only one in twenty is nonwhite. One in five is female.
Ninety-three percent of them have college degrees, and fifty-five percent have attended graduate school as well. Thus they are among the
best-educated people in this country. In addition, they may be in-

cluded among the most well-paid individuals in America. In 1978, 78 percent of them earned at least $30,000, and one in three had salaries exceeding $50,000.

In terms of geography, most are from the northern industrial states. In fact, two-fifths of them are from three states: New York, New Jersey, and Pennsylvania. Ten percent come from New England, one in five from Illinois, Indiana, Michigan, or Ohio. Only 3 percent come from the entire Pacific Coast, including California.[20]

One of the most disturbing characteristics about the members of the media elite is their secular outlook on life. According to Lichter and Rothman:

> Exactly 50 percent eschew any religious affiliation. Another 14 percent are Jewish, and almost one in four (23 percent) was raised in a Jewish household. Only one in five identifies himself as Protestant, and one in eight as Catholic. Very few are regular churchgoers. Only 8 percent go to church or synagogue weekly, and 86 percent seldom or never attend religious service.[21]

Politically, 54 percent identify themselves as left of center; only 19 percent placed themselves on the right of the political spectrum. "Of those who say they voted, the proportion of leading journalists who supported the Democratic presidential candidate never dropped below 80 percent. In 1972, when 62 percent of the electorate chose Nixon, 81 percent of the media elite voted for McGovern."[22] Lichter and Rothman reported that "in the Democratic landslide of 1964, media leaders picked Johnson over Goldwater by the staggering margin of sixteen-to-one or 94 to 6 percent."

By an overwhelming majority, the media elite are liberals and godless individuals who represent such a secular world view that they are totally neutral about God or are downright antagonistic to belief in God. "They show a strong preference for welfare capitalism, pressing for assistance to the poor in the form of income redistribution and guaranteed employment. Few are outright Socialists."

While most of the media elite believe in the free enterprise system, they also insist that the government should do much more to help the poor. "These attitudes," noted Lichter and Rothman, "mirror the traditional perspective of American liberals who—unlike many European social democrats—accept an essentially capitalistic economic framework, even as they press for expansion of the welfare state."[23]

"Leading journalists," observe these researchers, "emerge from our survey as strong supporters of environmental protection, affirmative action, women's rights, homosexual rights and sexual freedom in general."

In the area of personal morality, these people revealed a distinctly amoral or pragmatic view of life. Eighty-four percent of them rejected state regulation of sexual practices; 90 percent of them agreed that a woman should have the right to decide if she wants to kill her unborn child; 75 percent disagreed that homosexuality is wrong; 85 percent supported the right of homosexuals to teach in schools; 54 percent did not consider adultery wrong; and only 15 percent strongly agreed that extramarital affairs are immoral.[24]

In the interviews, Lichter and Rothman asked these media leaders to rate seven different groups according to their amount of influence or power in America. They offered the following list: black leaders, feminists, consumer groups, labor unions, business leaders, and the news media. Then the media leaders were asked to rate these groups according to the kind of power or influence *they* feel each should have.

The two charts below indicate how the media leaders rated these seven groups.

As you will notice in the first chart, they consider feminists to be the least powerful, followed by black leaders, intellectuals, and consumer groups. Unions ranked third, leaving media second only to business in terms of power in America.

When the media elite was asked to rate these groups in terms of their preferred hierarchy of influence (*see* Chart 2) business and union leaders were quickly demoted. Feminists moved up one notch, but blacks, intellectuals, and consumer groups would gain more influence than either business or labor. *"Emerging at the top of the heap, as the group most favored to direct American society, are the media."*[25]

It should be mentioned that when business leaders were asked to rate these seven groups, they placed themselves at the top as well. They also buried the media elite in the fifth position—exactly where the media would like to place business, if it could. As Lichter and Roth-

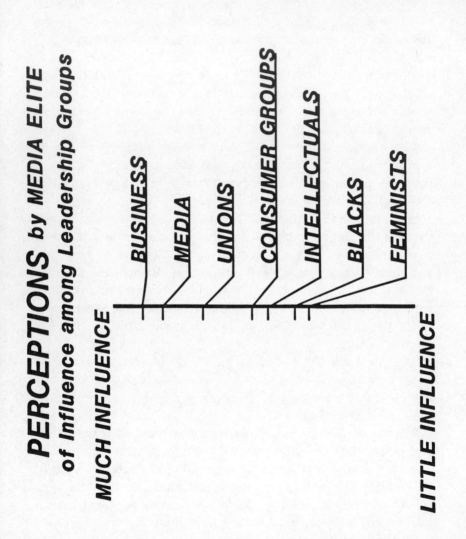

Chart 1

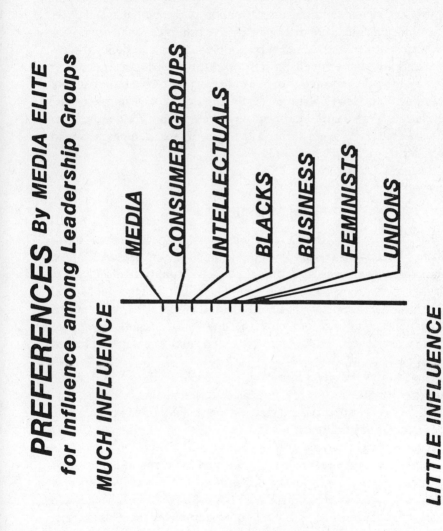

PREFERENCES *By MEDIA ELITE for Influence among Leadership Groups*

MUCH INFLUENCE

MEDIA

CONSUMER GROUPS

INTELLECTUALS

BLACKS

BUSINESS

FEMINISTS

UNIONS

LITTLE INFLUENCE

Chart 2

man noted, "Indeed, the hostility these two elites seem to feel toward each other is rather striking."[26]

After examining this report, can we really assume that those who control the media are a fair representation of the public at large? Or does this report indicate that our entire communications system is in the hands of men and women whose moral values and political commitments are totally at odds with those of the majority of Americans? Can we trust these people to give us honest news? Or are they simply imposing their views upon us? I really don't think we can rely on the media elite to give us a fair, balanced picture of the world around us. We are seeing the world through the eyes of liberal/humanists who consider religion to be irrelevant.

The Morality Gap

The Lichter and Rothman report on media perspectives offers a fascinating contrast to a recent study on the public's attitudes and values. This report, *The Connecticut Mutual Life Report on American Values in the 80s: The Impact of Belief,* was initiated by the Connecticut Mutual Life Insurance Company in an effort to determine the relevance of "traditional" values to our modern culture. The report "sought to identify the beliefs and attitudes of leaders, and to compare them to the public."[27]

The researchers surveyed over 1,600 people in the general public and nearly 1,800 leaders in the areas of business, education, government, law and justice, the military, the news media, religion, science, and voluntary associations.

What researchers discovered amazed them! They found that "the impact of religious belief reaches far beyond the realm of politics, and has penetrated virtually every dimension of American experience. This force is rapidly becoming a more powerful factor in American life than whether someone is liberal or conservative, male or female, young or old, or a blue-collar or white-collar worker."[28]

The study revealed that although less than half of those interviewed attended church regularly, 74 percent of them considered themselves to be religious.

Most shocking of all was the very clear "morality gap" that exists between the public and America's leaders. As the following list shows, the leaders tend to be far more liberal in their views than the general public. Take a look at these percentages:

	LEADERS	PUBLIC
Homosexuality is wrong	42%	71%
Abortion is immoral	36%	65%
Smoking marijuana is immoral	33%	57%
God loves them	54%	73%

According to the researchers, "Because leaders are among the less religious Americans, the study observes that they may be out of touch with the current of faith which appears to be gathering strength among the public in this decade."[29]

The report also made this very encouraging observation: "... It is the intensely religious who may well be the most vocal group in the eighties, just as it was the disenchanted who were the most vocal in the sixties and the seventies."[30] The media and government leaders are out of step with the people.

From this report and the Lichter and Rothman study, it is clear that our "leaders" and the media elite are out of step with the morality and values of the majority of the American people.

Whether a Hollywood producer, writer, or a news correspondent on the evening news, the majority of the people who create our television shows and convey our news are humanists who are anti-God and devoid of any absolute moral standards. By denying the need for absolute morality based upon the Word of God, these men and women are left without any way to truly judge whether something is right or wrong. They have become victims of "situation ethics," fashioning their morality as they go along. What may be "true" today may not be "true" tomorrow. Their morality is as changeable as clothing fashions.

Can we, as Christians, rely on these amoral individuals to provide us with reliable, factual news reporting or decent television viewing? Obviously we cannot. Is there anything we can do about this dilemma? Of course there is. Solutions will be discussed in a later chapter.

In the meantime, keep in mind that a person's belief in God influences everything he thinks or does. If he does not believe in a Supreme Being, he will reject moral absolutes and usually ridicule those who uphold them. The vicious attacks on the Moral Majority, or Religious Right, is just one evidence of the media's true beliefs. For that reason everything you read in the press or see and hear on TV and radio should be evaluated in the light of who is saying it and his basic beliefs. You cannot separate news, programming, or TV information from the philosophy of the person giving the information, whether related to abortion, homosexuality, pornography, criminal rights, welfare rights, the economy, or national defense. The reporter's belief or unbelief in God and His moral absolutes will influence what he presents and the way in which he presents it.

Who Are the Hidden Censors?

How did this happen? How did these liberal/humanists who are imposing their opinion on the rest of us gain such powerful control? Senator Barry Goldwater suggests two reasons in his book, *The Conscience of the Majority.*

One is based on the fact that many of today's veteran news correspondents were just cub reporters during the New Deal. Caught up in the ultraliberalism of the Roosevelt era, they learned quickly that if they wanted to make it big as journalists, they had to adopt a liberal viewpoint.

FDR was a master at exploiting these newsmen, using the press conference as a propaganda tool to push his own views. Many of the questions asked by reporters at these press conferences had been written by White House staff members and handed to FDR's favorite reporters. More independent-minded journalists were ridiculed by the president, and their questions went unanswered. The Roosevelt administration did its best to develop a group of journalists willing to consistently push the liberal lines.

As Goldwater observed, the New Deal:

> . . . Soon developed favorites among the reporters and these favorites became famous and extremely well paid because off their typewriters rolled the exclusive accounts of many new programs and new approaches which the Roosevelt government planned to take in the revamping of a nation's political and economic structure. . . . Many of the people who were cub reporters in those days and now are the pub-

lishers and editors of today were taught very early the value of adopt-
ing a liberal approach to their work.[1]

Another factor contributing to the rise of a liberal/humanist elite in
the media was the ascent of the organized labor movement. "It was in
this period," explained Goldwater, "that the American Newspaper
Guild gained its great power in the ranks of the nation's reporters. In
those days, becoming a member of the newspaper guild almost automatically aligned a reporter with the overall objective of organized
labor. . . . This of course, was during the popular reign of a noted
newspaper leftist and columnist named Heywood Broun. Mr. Broun,
as president of the Guild and as a newspaper columnist, very often
called the tune for a biased and slanted orchestration on the part of liberal members of the Fourth Estate."[2]

Heywood Broun was one of the most widely read columnists in
America during the 1930s. His column appeared regularly in the *New
York Telegram* from 1928 through 1939 and was syndicated by the
Scripps-Howard newspaper chain. Broun was the major force behind
the founding of the American Newspaper Guild and served as its pres-
ident from 1933 to 1939.[3]

An openly admitted Fabian Socialist, Broun was successful in radi-
calizing and manipulating the liberal journalists who joined his
American Newspaper Guild. Liberals, of course, have always been
victimized by hard-core radicals in the news media. They easily fall
victim to Marxist thinking because liberals share so many of their
convictions and ideals.

By contrast, Howard K. Smith, a liberal journalist, is willing to criticize his fellow journalists for their biases. In an interview with Edith
Efron, Smith commented, "Many of my colleagues have the depth of a
saucer. They cling to the tag 'liberal' that grew popular in the time of
Franklin Roosevelt, even though they've forgotten its content. . . . They
don't know what they stand for any more, and they're hunting for a
new voice to give them new bearings."[4]

The "new voice" the liberals have found, says Smith, is the New
Left. Smith observes, "They want to cling to the label 'liberal,' and
they cling to those who seem strong—namely, the New Left. The New
Left shouts tirades, rather than offering reasoned arguments. People

bow down to them, so they have come to seem strong, to *seem* sure of themselves. As a result, there's a gravitation to them by the liberals who *are not* sure of themselves. This has given the New Left grave power over the old Left."[5]

Soviet Exploitation of the Media

Unfortunately, we are not just being manipulated by liberal do-gooders in the media. There is considerable evidence that the media—including film, print, and television—have long been the target of Soviet infiltration and disinformation campaigns. In addition, the Council on Foreign Relations and its offspring, the Trilateral Commission have both exercised an inordinate control over what we are allowed to see, read, and hear in America (*see* page 178).

The media in America have been—and continue to be—the target of Soviet agents. The Soviets have sought to conquer America not just with military might, but through a cleverly planned, long-range psychological-warfare campaign. They are engaged in a propaganda war, intending to confuse and demoralize America until we finally suffer what amounts to a national psychological breakdown.

To accomplish this goal, they have sought to infiltrate and use every medium outlet in America. This campaign has been going on ever since the Bolshevik Revolution, in 1917. Within two years, radical Communists had founded the American Communist Party (in September of 1919), and the infiltration and subversion of the United States had begun in earnest.

The Communists knew that if they were going to have any impact in America, they would have to worm their way into the media. In 1913 Soviet Foreign Minister Molotov prepared a report for the Politburo (the principal policy-making committee of the Communist Party, USSR) in which he urged Communists to make use of non-Communist newspapers to spread Communist propaganda.[6]

Igor Bogolepov was a high official in the Foreign Ministry before he defected to the West in the 1940s. In testimony before the Senate Internal Security Subcommittee in 1952, he paraphrased Molotov's report in these words: "Who reads the Communist papers? Only a few people who are already Communists. We don't need to propagandize them. What is our object? Who do we have to influence? We have to influence non-Communists if we want to make them Communists or if we want to fool them. So we have to try to infiltrate in the big press, to influence millions of people, and not merely hundreds of thousands."[7]

To train Communist agents to infiltrate the media and other centers of influence in non-Communist nations, the Soviets established the Lenin School in Moscow in 1926. Its sole purpose was to train non-Soviet Communists to betray their countries. Since 1926 this propaganda training school has graduated more than 120,000 agents—men and women who have returned to their native lands to serve Soviet purposes.[8]

Soviet Disinformation Campaigns

When Yuri Andropov was head of the KGB (Soviet secret police), he upgraded the KGB's Department D (Disinformation) into a "service," renaming it Directorate A. He placed great importance on this particular work of the KGB. He realized that spreading lying propaganda about America and other Western nations could be just as destructive as using military force.[9]

Directorate A is given the task of planting phony stories in the Western news media. It uses its own Soviet agents or men and women who have been duped into helping carry out Soviet objectives in the press.

The KGB uses several types of journalists to spread Soviet propaganda. One is called a *maggot,* not pro-Soviet but a pragmatist, he will write whatever will get him promoted. Then there is the *termite*—a left-winger who willingly supports Communist objectives.

A *mole* is a dedicated Communist. He infiltrates the media, remaining politically inactive for years as he works his way up the ladder within the organization. All the while, he is carefully writing stories that promote Soviet objectives.

A man who is intimately familiar with Soviet exploitation of the media is Dr. Igor S. Glagolev, formerly chief of the Disarmament Section of the Institute of World Economic and International Relations, USSR Academy of Sciences. Glagolev defected to the United States in 1976.

How do the Soviets use the media? "Sometimes they use journalists who are in favor of Communism already," reported Glagolev. "They give them materials. Sometimes they bribe them and they pay certain journalists for their stories. . . . Sometimes it is very easy to see that certain journalists *always* support the Communist line—*always.* So, if you read their articles, it is quite clear that somehow they are connected with the leadership of the Soviet Union. Of course they try to use Western terms, Western ideas, about democracy, peace, detente; but they *always* support the Soviet line and suggestions."[10]

Whittaker Chambers was also familiar with how Communists use the media. The late Chambers became a dedicated Communist in the 1920s and by 1932 had become a Soviet spy, receiving top-secret government documents from Alger Hiss and other Communist agents within our government. According to Chambers, "There is probably no important magazine or newspaper in the country that is not Communist-penetrated to some degree."[11]

Walter Duranty

One of the most successful pro-Soviet propagandists for the *New York Times* was Walter Duranty. Curtis MacDougall identified Duranty to his journalism students as one of the "best journalistic scholars" who ever lived.

Duranty, a foreign correspondent for the *Times* from 1913 through 1939, spent from 1921 until 1939 as the *Times* Moscow correspondent. For nearly twenty years Duranty faithfully followed Soviet objectives in his news dispatches.

He was in Moscow during the Stalinist purge trials and the mass starvation of some 6 to 7 million farmers in the Ukraine—farmers who were deliberately starved to death under the authority of Nikita Khrushchev. Yet Duranty always maintained that all was well in the Soviet Union. He once called Stalin "the greatest living statesman." In his own biography, *I Write As I Please,* published in 1935, Duranty declared, "Looking backward over the fourteen years I have spent in Russia, I cannot escape the conclusion that this period has been a heroic chapter in the life of Humanity."[12]

Journalists Eugene Lyons and Malcolm Muggeridge were stationed in Moscow at the same time Duranty was there. According to Mug-

geridge, no journalist followed the Soviet party line closer than
Duranty in his news reports. In fact, Muggeridge noted that Soviet officials were always upholding Duranty as the ideal Western journalist.
"It, of course, suited his material interests thus to write everything the
Soviet authorities wanted him to," said Muggeridge, "that collectivi-
zation of agriculture was working well, with no famine conditions anywhere; that the purges were justified, the confessions genuine, and the
judicial procedure impeccable."

Muggeridge continued, "If the *New York Times* went on all those
years giving great prominence to Duranty's messages, building him
and them up when they were so evidently nonsensically untrue, to the
point that he came to be accepted as the great Russian expert in
America, and played a major part in shaping President Roosevelt's
policies vis-a-vis the USSR—this was not, we may be sure, because the
Times was deceived. Rather because it *wanted* to be so deceived, and
Duranty provided the requisite deception material."

Muggeridge went on to note, "Since his time, there have been a
whole succession of others fulfilling this same role—in Cuba, in Vietnam, in Latin America. It is an addiction, and in such cases there is
never any lack of hands to push in the needle and give the fix. Just as
the intelligentsia have been foremost in the struggle to abolish intelligence, so the great organs of capitalism like the *New York Times* have
spared no expense or effort to ensure that capitalism will not survive."[13]

Herbert L. Matthews and Fidel Castro

Journalist Herbert L. Matthews, a reporter for the *New York Times*
from 1922 to 1967, was, according to Fidel Castro's sister Juanita (who
fled to the United States after the Communist takeover), one of Fidel's
best friends in America.

Juanita Castro testified before the Committee on Un-American Activities, House of Representatives, on June 11, 1965. In the hearing,
Congressman Joe Pool asked her: "Miss Castro, is it within your direct
knowledge as to whom Castro has considered his most ardent supporters in the United States?"

Miss Castro answered, "On different occasions I heard Fidel personally mention as his greatest friends in the United States Messrs. Herbert Matthews, Carleton Beals, and Waldo Frank.

"On the several trips that Mr. Matthews has taken to Cuba, he has been constantly accompanied by the Cuban security police.

"During Mr. Herbert Matthews' many trips to Cuba, he has never tried to get close to the workingman to ask him what the real conditions are in Cuba, and yet when he returns to the United States, he publishes only that which he thinks is convenient or helpful for the Communist regime."[14]

Castro had been a ruthless Marxist hoodlum since his days as a student at the University of Havana. While at the university, he earned the nickname *Bola de Churre,* "Ball of Dirty Grease." Castro became head of a student terrorist organization and used machine guns to kill the ex-president of the University Student Federation and a friend, Carlos Pucho Samper.

In 1948 he and other Communist agents flew into Bogota, Colombia, to foment an insurrection. By the time Castro and his thugs had finished, over 1,000 people were dead and 136 major buildings had been burned to the ground.[15]

According to W. Cleon Skousen, Castro was known to be a Soviet agent even before he arrived in Colombia, "Alberto Nino, Security Chief of Colombia, published a book in 1949 on the insurrection. He has much to say about Fidel Castro. Nino describes how Castro and Rafael del Pino were put under surveillance the moment they arrived at the airport. 'These two men came as replacements for two Russian agents stationed in Cuba, whose plans were known and who were expected by the Colombian police.' "[16]

Yet in spite of overwhelming and well-publicized evidence that Fidel Castro was a Communist revolutionary, Herbert L. Matthews, gaining a personal interview with Castro, likened him in his articles to Abraham Lincoln. The rest of the news media began puffing Castro as the Robin Hood of Cuba—instead of a Marxist terrorist supported by the Soviet Union.

Fidel Castro denied being a Communist until he finally seized power. Since that time, we know what has happened in Cuba. Thousands of anti-Communists were imprisoned, killed, and tortured. Cuba has become a Soviet military base, exporting arms and guerrillas throughout Central and South America. And in November, 1982 four of Castro's top aides were indicted by a federal grand jury in Miami of conspiring to ship marijuana and methaqualone into the United States. It is Castro's objective to destroy our society by encouraging widespread drug abuse.

El Salvador and Ray Bonner

Raymond Bonner, now on the *Times* staff in New York City, acted as a correspondent in El Salvador. A lawyer by training, not a journalist, Bonner spent time working with Ralph Nader and the Consumers Union.

Reed Irvine, publisher of the excellent *AIM Report* has been doing battle with the *Times* and other establishment media outlets for their left-leaning bias. His organization, Accuracy in Media, has done massive research into Ray Bonner's reporting of events in El Salvador.

Reed Irvine feels that Ray Bonner has been worth a division of Communist troops to the El Salvadoran Communist guerrillas. Indeed he has. Daniel James, distinguished journalist and expert on Central America, analyzed the content of fifty-one stories written by Bonner for the *Times* during the first half of 1982.[17] According to James, "It is evident . . . that one of his main objectives was to discredit the government and the military forces that were standing in the way of a Communist takeover of El Salvador. At the same time, he sought to portray the Communist-backed guerrillas favorably. One thing that Bonner has refused to do is label the guerrillas as Marxists. He explained in a symposium at the Center for the Study of Democratic Institutions, 'I have always stayed away from calling groups Marxist-led, because I don't know exactly what that means.' Bonner usually simply uses the terms 'rebels' or 'guerrillas,' but he says, even 'calling them "guerrillas" has negative connotations.' For that matter, he says, 'calling them "leftists" . . . has negative connotations.' "[18]

Bonner's story in the January 11, 1982 issue of the *Times* claimed that American advisers had watched El Salvadoran soldiers torture two teenagers. The source for this story came from a young Salvadoran army deserter living in Mexico. The story was never corroborated by anyone else, yet the *Times* gave the story prominent play on page two.[19]

After Reed Irvine confronted *Times* editors with the facts, the editors finally admitted that the story had been "overplayed." Mr. Sulzberger explained, "Frankly, I think we overplayed the story since it was based solely on the unverified statement of one soldier."[20] Yet the damage was done—the Salvadoran army was made to look like Nazi storm troopers.

The nation of El Salvador has not yet—at this writing—been destroyed by Soviet disinformation campaigns in the American press. But it may only be a matter of time before the Communist dupes and willing agents succeed in choking off American military assistance to El Salvador. If—or when—El Salvador falls into Communist hands, we can again thank the *Times* for contributing to that nation's demise.

The *New York Times* has not been alone in its disinformation campaign against anti-Communist governments, for the major TV networks have also done their part. Interestingly enough, it was *Times* reporter Philip Taubman who wrote about guerrilla exploitation of the media in an article that appeared in the February 26, 1982 issue. Taubman quoted two terrorists, Hector Oqueli and Ruben Zamora, as saying that they were determined to destroy El Salvador by using the American media. " 'We have to win the war inside the United States,' said Hector Oqueli, one of the rebel leaders . . . His colleague, Ruben Zamora, added, 'We have tried to change our public image.' "

According to Taubman:

> One step was to invite American reporters in El Salvador to visit rebel strongholds in the countryside. These visits, which began late last year, generated a series of newspaper articles about the rebels and their supporters.
>
> At the same time, the leaders began to contact editorial writers at major American newspapers, hoping to persuade them to write more sympathetically about the insurgents.
>
> The most important papers, according to Mr. Zamora, are the New York Times, The Washington Post, the Los Angeles Times, the Miami Herald, the Wall Street Journal, The Boston Globe and The Chicago Tribune. . . . The rebels said they are considering using a computer to store and organize the names of reporters and editors in the United States with whom they have regular dealings.[21]

The Communist terrorists should rejoice. The networks are now helping to destroy El Salvador as well. The Public Broadcasting Network aired a proguerrilla show called "El Salvador: Another Vietnam" in January, 1981. CBS did a hatchet job on El Salvador in its documentary, "Central America in Revolt" in March, 1982. During the summer of 1982, PBS aired another anti-El Salvador documentary called "Roses in December," relating the story of the murder of Jean Donovan and three nuns. The ads placed in local newspapers pictured a vicious El Salvadoran soldier getting ready to shoot Donovan in the back of the head.[22]

The disinformation campaign will continue until El Salvador becomes another Communist dictatorship. The journalists who helped destroy the nation will then find new assignments in other Central American countries, and the disinformation campaign will start anew.

Robert Minor and World Communism

Few Americans in this generation have even heard of Robert Minor, yet I believe he had a profound impact on the advance of Communism in America. In 1918 Robert Minor was a reporter for the *New York World,* the *Philadelphia Public Ledger,* and Max Eastman's *Liberator.* He traveled to Russia and somehow gained the confidence of Lenin and Trotsky, even securing an exclusive interview with Lenin published in the *New York World.*[23]

Minor was no naive, nonpolitical reporter. He spent nine months in Russia, learning about Bolshevism from Lenin and Trotsky. Later he traveled to Germany and was arrested by United States military police for spreading pro-Communist propaganda among the American soldiers stationed in Europe.

If justice had been carried out, Robert Minor would have been tried for treason and executed by firing squad. But Minor had garnered powerful allies within the United States government. At one point he had gained a long, private interview with Colonel Edward Mandell House, in Paris. House, originator of the Council on Foreign Relations, was Woodrow Wilson's closest personal assistant and member of the American Peace Delegation in Paris. For reasons that have never been fully explained, House had Minor released.[24]

A man well acquainted with Minor was Benjamin Gitlow, one of the original founders of the Communist Party, USA. Gitlow repudiated Communism in the 1930s and published an expose of Communism, called *The Whole of Their Lives,* in 1948. According to Gitlow, "From the Bolshevik standpoint, Robert Minor is the most important figure in American Communism, for he has done more than any other American Communist, living or dead, to transform the American Communist movement into a real Bolshevik movement."[25]

It was journalist Minor who taught his American comrades to reject any moral values that would stand in the way of accomplishing Soviet objectives in America. Gitlow said of him, ". . . In his efforts to develop a Bolshevik mentality in the American Communists, he wrote: 'Honesty is a bourgeois virtue.' From this it logically followed that to lie, to be dishonest was a Communist virtue. The diabolical ethical code was not Minor's invention. It was, and still is, the code of Bolshevism. Getting the American Communists to reject the ethical concepts of civilization constituted the central point in the campaign for the Bolshevization of the American Communists."[26]

The Council on Foreign Relations and the Trilateral Commission

In 1970 W. Cleon Skousen published *The Naked Capitalist.* This book is actually a 143-page *book review* of a monumental work entitled *Tragedy and Hope,* written by the late Dr. Carroll Quigley. In its opening page we read the following:

> "I think the Communist conspiracy is merely a branch of a much bigger conspiracy."
> The above statement was made to this reviewer several years ago by Dr. Bella Dodd, a former member of the National Committee of the Unites States Communist Party. . . .
> Dr. Dodd said she first became aware of some mysterious super leadership right after World War II when the U.S. Communist Party had difficulty getting instructions from Moscow on several vital matters requiring immediate attention. The American Communist hierarchy was told that any time they had an emergency of this kind they should contact any one of three designated persons at the Waldorf

Towers. Dr. Dodd noted that whenever the Party obtained instructions from any of these three men, Moscow always ratified them.

What puzzled Dr. Dodd was the fact that not one of these three contacts was a Russian. Nor were any of them Communists. In fact, all three were extremely wealthy American capitalists!

Dr. Dodd said, "I would certainly like to find out who is really running things."[27]

That is one of the main reasons I have written this book, to point out who is really running things, particularly in the mass media.

We must begin with a look at the Council on Foreign Relations.

The CFR was the brainchild of Colonel Edward Mandell House, close personal advisor to President Woodrow Wilson from 1913 through 1919. In 1912 House had written a fictional account of a socialist takeover of America called *Philip Dru: Administrator*. In this book, penned anonymously, he laid out his own personal plan for converting America into a socialist dictatorship. And while he was Wilson's advisor, he set about to accomplish his goal.[28]

But House had far bigger plans than simply turning America into a socialist dictatorship. He was interested in bringing about a world government. In 1916 House brought together a so-called brain trust of men to draw up plans for a world government under the control of the League of Nations.

In order to prepare the public for acceptance of membership in the League of Nations/world government, House set up a secret meeting in Paris to form an organization that would spearhead the propaganda drive. Along with him were Walter Lippmann, Christian Herter, Allen W. Dulles, and John Foster Dulles. From this meeting came two organizations, one British, the other American. On the British side was the Institute for International Affairs; in America it was called the Council on Foreign Relations. Both groups had the same objective in mind: establishing a world government to be ruled by the superrich.

In writing *Tragedy and Hope,* Dr. Carroll Quigley did conservatives a great favor by carefully explaining exactly how this Anglo-American conspiracy operates. Quigley did not write his book to condemn the one-worlders, but to praise them for the part they have played in world history. He explains, "I know of the operations of this network because

I have studied it for twenty years and was permitted for two years, in the early 1960s, to examine its papers and secret records, I have no aversion to it or to most of its aims and have, for much of my life, been close to it and to many of its instruments. I have objected, both in the past and recently, to a few of its policies ... but in general my chief difference of opinion is that it wishes to remain unknown, and I believe its role in history is significant enough to be known."[29]

According to Quigley, the founders of this Anglo-American "establishment" were determined to institute a worldwide dictatorship in the hands of an elite group of bankers and industrialists. These elitists realized, of course, that they had to seize control of the mass communications media if they were to succeed with their plans. They certainly couldn't allow a free press to exist. They accomplished this by buying up newspapers and magazines and planting their own CFR agents in editorial positions. According to Quigley, "Much of its influence [is] through five American newspapers [The *New York Times, New York Herald Tribune, Christian Science Monitor, Washington Post,* and the lamented *Boston Evening Transcript*].[30] Erwin Canham, longtime editor of the *Christian Science Monitor,* was an early member of the Council on Foreign Relations and served this Anglo-American establishment as the anonymous American correspondent for *The Round Table,* a quarterly magazine published by one-worlders in Britain.

Quigley states:

> The two ends of this English-speaking axis have sometimes been called, perhaps facetiously, the English and American Establishments. There is, however, a considerable degree of truth behind the joke, a truth which reflects a very real power structure. It is this power structure which the radical right in the United States has been attacking for years in the belief that they were attacking the Communists. This is particularly true when these attacks are directed, as they so frequently are, at "Harvard socialism," or at "Left-wing newspapers" like the *New York Times,* and the *Washington Post.*[31]
>
> There does exist, and has existed for a generation, an international Anglophile network which operates, to some extent, in the way the radical right believes the Communists act. In fact, this network ... has no aversion to cooperating with the Communists, or any other group, and frequently does so.[32]

The CFR and World Dictatorship

Does the CFR really desire to bring about a one-world government? According to Admiral Chester Ward, the majority of CFR members "visualize the utopian submergence of the United States as a subsidiary administrative unit of a global government...."[33]

Of parallel interest, both *Humanist Manifesto I,* published in 1933, and *Humanist Manifesto II,* published in 1973, call for a world government as well, ruled by themselves—godless, amoral humanists.

In *Humanist Manifesto II* we read, "We deplore the division of humankind on nationalistic grounds. We have reached a turning point in human history where the best option is to *transcend the limits of national sovereignty* and to move toward the building of a world community in which all sectors of the human family can participate. Thus we look to the development of a system of world law and a world order based upon transnational federal government."[34]

The CFR had hoped that the United Nations would be the structure to impose this new world order upon us. But in recent years the UN has fallen into disfavor. Thus there are new ways of entangling America in a world dictatorship.

In the April 1974 issue of CFR journal, *Foreign Affairs,* Professor Richard N. Gardner wrote an article entitled, "The Hard Road to World Order." In it he admits that it is unrealistic to expect America to jump into world government through the UN. But there is a better way, he advises, calling "for an end to run around national sovereignty, eroding it piece by piece."[35]

How is this to be accomplished? By involving America in restrictive alliances and international agreements through such world organizations as the International Monetary Fund, the World Bank, the Law of the Sea Conference, the World Food Conference, the World Population Conference, and similar bodies.

Conservative journalist Dan Smoot, a former FBI agent, was one of the first men in America to do an in-depth study of the Council on Foreign Relations and its affiliated one-world organizations. In 1962 he published the results of his study, *The Invisible Government.* He managed to put together an extensive list of CFR members who had gained influential positions within our government, educational system, news media, and other centers of influence in our society.

Building upon the work of Smoot, Phyllis Schlafly and Admiral Chester Ward wrote *Kissinger on the Couch* in 1975. Ward has had the advantage of observing the workings of the CFR from the *inside,* for he has been a member. According to Ward, there are several warring factions within the CFR, but none of them loses sight of the ultimate goal of world government.

A small but immensely powerful faction within the CFR is comprised of international bankers and their agents. According to Ward, "Primarily, they want the world banking monopoly from whatever power ends up in control of the global government. They would probably prefer that this be an all-powerful United Nations organization; but they are also prepared to deal with and for a one-world government controlled by the Soviet Communists if U.S. sovereignty is ever surrendered to them."[36]

To the CFR members, therefore, it really matters little which power bloc ends up controlling the one-world government. They expect to be sitting on top of the dictatorship, regardless of who ultimately seizes power.

The Trilateral Commission and World Government

To help establish world government "piece by piece," David Rockefeller, head of the CFR, organized the Trilateral Commission in 1973. The purpose of this commission is to form a powerful alliance between Western Europe, Japan, and North America, intertwining the policies of each power center to such an extent that American sovereignty will eventually be destroyed and our nation will become one province in a worldwide slave state.

Rockefeller apparently received inspiration for founding the Trilateral Commission after reading the book *Between Two Ages* by Zbigniew Brzezinski. In this book, Brzezinski declares that America is obsolete and needs a centrally managed economic system. He also believes that America must align itself with other nations and should give up national sovereignty. "The desire to create one larger, formal state," says Brzezinski, "is itself an extension of reasoning derived from the age of nationalism. It makes much more sense to attempt to associate existing states through a variety of indirect ties and already developing limitations on national sovereignty."

Brzezinski goes on to say, "Movement toward such a community will in all probability require two broad and overlapping phases. The first of these would involve the forging of community links among the United States, Western Europe, and Japan, as well as with other more advanced countries (for example, Australia, Israel, Mexico). The second phase would include the extension of these links to more advanced communist countries."[37] Little wonder David Rockefeller chose Brzezinski to head the Trilateral Commission.

When one reads CFR and Trilateral Commission documents and analyzes the writings of CFR and Trilateral Commission members, it is clear beyond any reasonable doubt that these two organizations are actively seeking to destroy our nation and establish a ruthless world dictatorship—to be run by them.

4

American Plurality in the Eighties

Whenever I have the opportunity to debate with secular humanists and we begin to discuss biblical morality, the subject of "pluralism" invariably comes up. The humanists ask, "Don't you know we live in a pluralistic society? You have no right to impose your particular view of morality upon the rest of us. Our moral values are just as valid as yours."

Just what is *pluralism* anyway? I find considerable confusion about the meaning of the word. To a liberal or humanist it means one thing; to a Christian or conservative it means something else. It is important that we understand the significance of the word—especially from a humanist viewpoint—because humanists use it to impose their moral anarchy upon all of us.

The *Webster's New Collegiate Dictionary* gives several definitions for *pluralism.* By quoting the definitions, we may clear up some of the misunderstandings:

> 3a: a theory that there are more than one or more than two kinds of ultimate reality b: a theory that reality is composed of a plurality of entities 4a: a state of society in which members of diverse ethnic, racial, religious, or social groups maintain an autonomous participation in and development of their traditional culture or special interest within the confines of a common civilization b: a concept, doctrine, or policy advocating this state.

When a liberal or humanist talks about pluralism he is predicating two or more "realities." To the humanist there are no moral absolutes.

Since morality is man-made, it can be whatever we choose it to be. In denying God as the true reality and final authority in all areas of life, liberals and humanists are dependent upon their own intellects to determine the nature of "reality," or what is moral, good, and true.

On the other hand, to a Christian or conservative, *pluralism* suggests a society of various ethnic, racial, social, and religious groups, living together in relative harmony, each group respecting the rights of the others.

So you see, the two contrasting groups are not operating from the same definition. If we are to understand and effectively counter amoral liberals, we must understand what *they* mean by *pluralism*.

The Foundations of American Freedom

Historically, America has always been proud of its pluralistic heritage—of being a "melting pot" for European immigrants who sailed to America in search of freedom and prosperity. Ours was a land of opportunity, a country of new beginnings for the oppressed peoples of Europe. From 1790 to 1921, when immigration quotas were imposed, over 40 million immigrants flocked to the United States.

In the beginning, America was colonized by men and women who had a deep commitment to the Lord Jesus Christ. As the *Mayflower* was anchored off the coast of Massachusetts in 1620, the men on that ship signed the Mayflower Compact, pledging their loyalty to King James and declaring that they had come to America "for the glory of God, and advancement of the Christian faith."

Most of these first settlers originated from northern Europe. They had been deeply influenced by the Reformation and based all their decisions upon the Word of God. They believed in an orderly world and in God-ordained moral absolutes.

Their influence was felt in the formation of the young nation. The Declaration of Independence, though written largely by Thomas Jefferson, a Unitarian, proudly declared: "We hold these truths to be self-evident, that all men are created equal, that they are endowed by their Creator with certain unalienable rights, that among these are Life, Liberty, and the pursuit of Happiness. . . ."

Our nation was founded on the firm belief that God is the author of life, the author of morality, the author of truth. There was no humanistic view of "pluralism"—two or more separate "realities"—in their world view. Only one truth and one reality was admitted: Jesus Christ, who declared that He was the way, the truth and the life.

Our Founding Fathers realized that because God is the author of freedom, government must be the servant, not the master over man. That is why they gave us a constitutional republic with a written constitution severely limiting the power of the federal government. The Bill of Rights, of course, was written to protect all Americans from the encroachments of the federal government on the rights of individuals and states. The Tenth Amendment declares it clearly: "The powers not delegated to the United States by the Constitution, nor prohibited by it to the States, are reserved to the States respectively, or to the people."

The Founding Fathers knew that because man is basically sinful, freedom in America could only be preserved by a Constitution that limited the powers of government. They recognized that freedom was a divine right, given by Almighty God to all men. It was not a privilege to be handed out by an all-powerful central government.

They also realized that no nation can long survive without sound religious principles undergirding the political system. George Washington affirmed this belief in his Farewell Address: "Of all the dispositions and habits which lead to political prosperity, religion and morality are indispensable supports. Reason and experience both forbid us to expect that natural morality can prevail in exclusion of Religious Principles."

In April of 1799, Dr. Jedediah Morse explained the connection between Christian principles and freedom.

> To the kindly influence of Christianity we owe that degree of civil freedom and political and social happiness which mankind now enjoys. In proportion as the genuine efforts of Christians are diminished in any nation, either through unbelief, or the corruption of its doctrines, or the neglect of its institutions; in the same proportion will the people of that nation recede from the blessings of genuine liberty, and appropriate the miseries of complete despotism.[1]

From its founding, America has been a religious nation. In fact, in the case involving the *Church of the Holy Trinity* v. *United States,* in

1892, the Supreme Court examined America's historical documents and concluded that, "This United States is a religious people. This is historically true. From the discovery of America to this hour there is a single voice making this affirmation."[2]

The Drift Toward Liberal Humanism

After about 1848, America began to lose its distinctively religious character, drifting toward liberal humanism. During the latter part of the nineteenth century, immigrants still flocked to the United States, but they did not share the Reformation view of the world held by the earlier colonizers. Yet they, too, sought freedom in this new land, which secures religious liberty uniformly. As Dr. Francis Schaeffer points out, "Thus, as we stand for religious freedom today, we need to realize that this must include a general religious freedom from the control of the state for all religions. It will not mean just freedom for those who are Christian."[3]

Historically, when men spoke of pluralism in America, they meant that America was a nation of diverse nationalities and religions. Regardless of race, social group, or creed, these immigrants were all guaranteed certain rights under our Constitution. Freedom of religion was among the most important of those.

The First Amendment had stated, "Congress shall make no law respecting an establishment of religion or prohibiting the free exercise thereof." The Founding Fathers wanted to assure that no state church would ever be established in America. They had experienced too many abuses from the Church of England or the Roman Catholic Church to permit a national church here. Yet they also desired to make it perfectly clear that they wanted no laws prohibiting the people from freely exercising their religious beliefs.

Unfortunately, times have changed. Humanists and liberals now use the First Amendment to destroy religious freedom in America. They have successfully thrown religious principles out of our public schools, and they are aggressively challenging private Christian schools as well.

During the early years of the twentieth century, the humanists wormed their way into our media, our educational system, the government, major foundations, and even many main-line churches. They started to attack traditional Christian morality and—until recently—had been rapidly converting our Christian nation into a secularized, inhuman state.

Humanists deny the existence of God, claiming that man is his own god. As I pointed out in my books *The Battle for the Mind* and *The Battle for the Family,* humanism is the greatest danger facing our nation today. I hold humanists responsible for the dreadful increase in venereal disease in our country, the rise of sexual perversion, the aborting of millions of babies, the escalating crime rate, and practically every social evil facing our society today. If we look behind each social problem in America, we will find a secular humanist thinker or theorist.

Now don't misunderstand. Many humanists and their more numerous cohorts, humanistic thinkers, are not necessarily subversive. I am not implying that they are purposely trying to increase the crime rate, accelerate the incidence of forcible rape, or premeditatedly render our streets unsafe after dark. I am saying, however, that the natural conclusions of humanist theory lead to the breakdown in law and order, legitimate authority, and ultimately in society itself.

I blame secular humanism for the vast majority of the social ills of our day. The fact that John Dewey's progressive education has deteriorated education or that "Earl Warren's Court" and Justice Douglas's impact on abortion, pornography, and other atheistic conclusions has deteriorated our quality of life in this country is not the less painful to 227 million Americans because those men did it honestly as secular-humanist thinkers.

Humanism Defined

What is humanism? It is far more than just a philosophy of life. It represents a militant religious system based upon five assumptions: atheism, evolution, amorality, the autonomous man, and a socialist world view.

God Denied. First and foremost, a humanist is an atheist. He proudly denies the existence of a Supreme Being. In the preface to the *Humanist Manifesto II,* Paul Kurtz and Edwin H. Wilson write that a belief in

God is an "... unproved and outmoded faith. Salvationism, based on mere affirmation, still appears as harmful, diverting people with false hopes of heaven hereafter. Reasonable minds look to other means for survival."[4]

Accident of Nature: Man.   Second, the humanist is an evolutionist. He believes that the universe is self-existent and than man is simply an accident of nature. Man is no different from a plant or a toad; he simply has more intelligence. The humanist also believes in the natural goodness of man.

The Make-It-Up-as-You-Go Morality.   Third, the humanist is amoral. That is, he assumes that moral concepts—ideas of good and evil, right and wrong—are man-made ideas, subject to change. No absolutes exist for him. That is why he so easily champions human dignity on one hand and then advocates abortion, infanticide, euthanasia, and the so-called "right" to suicide on the other. As a pragmatist, the humanist makes up his morality as he goes along. When he gets into government, he lacks a strict code of ethics. He creates law based upon what suits him at that particular moment.

One dedicated humanist who carried the humanist religion to its logical conclusion is the late Walter Kaufmann, a Princeton professor. In his book, *Without Guilt and Justice,* published in 1973, he deals with these two concepts. According to the eminent Christian scholar Dr. Rousas J. Rushdoony, Kaufmann "... held that guilt and justice are theological concepts and hence no longer valid, if there be no God, there is neither good nor evil, nor guilt and innocence. And the idea of justice is a myth. Not all humanists are as honest as Kaufmann was, and as a result, the concept of justice has been retained as a facade for the perspectives of humanism."[5]

Without the firm foundation of God's Word guiding our actions, there is no way we can determine what is really right or wrong. If morality is man-made, then any form of behavior is normal. That is why humanists gladly support drug use, sexual perversion, baby killing, suicide—in short, any behavior that supposedly "frees" man from the "repressive" restraints of Christian morality. The humanist tolerates any behavior and any idea—except Christianity. He will defend the "rights" of murderers, homosexuals, drug pushers, child pornographers, Communist spies, and terrorists. He is "tolerant" of every form of degeneracy known to man—but he despises Christian morality. Suddenly the believer has no rights, and he must be silenced at all costs. He has no right to speak in public, no right to his own private schools. He will be mercilessly censored, ridiculed, and jailed for daring to preach the Gospel of Christ or take an active role in our society.

Man Is God. The fourth basic tenet of humanism concerns the idea of the autonomous man. In *Humanist Manifesto II,* the writers state, "We reject all religious, ideological, or moral codes that denigrate the individual, suppress freedom, dull intellect, dehumanize personality. We believe in maximum individual autonomy consonant with social responsibility."[6]

Auto means "self" and *nomos* means "law." In other words, the humanist makes his own laws to govern his behavior. Yet the Bible tells us clearly and repeatedly that when man does not obey the laws of God, he is in rebellion and sin. The humanists, however, are arrogantly lawless. They fashion a make-it-up-as-you-go morality. The humanist philosophy can be summed up in a few words: "If it feels good, do it."

A One-World Government. The fifth tenet of humanism is a socialist one-world view. A dedicated humanist is an internationalist first, an American second. He looks to all-powerful government as the savior of mankind. In his thinking, only a benevolent world government will bring true peace to the world.

You will always find humanists in the forefront of the push for a "new world order" (their euphemism for a ruthless world dictatorship ruled by a humanist elite). As stated in *Humanist Manifesto II,* the humanists ". . . look to the development of a system of world law and a world order based upon transnational federal government."[7]

As you can see, every tenet of humanism is diametrically opposed to Judeo-Christian principles and is blatantly anti-American. Humanism is the deadly enemy of the Christian church, of America, and of human freedom.

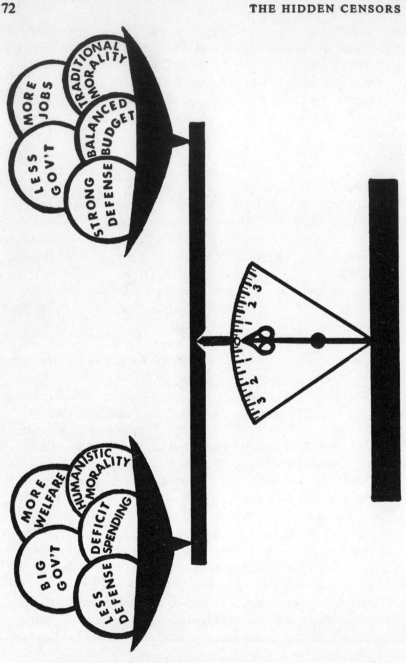

Humanism Will Lead to a Police State

When a humanist speaks about pluralism, he is just trying to justify the imposition of his amorality upon our nation. As the English historian E. R. Norman once observed, "Pluralism is a word society employs during the transition from one orthodoxy to another."[8] It is the objective of humanism to replace orthodox Christianity with secular humanism. Whether or not humanists realize it, the end result will be anarchy, followed by a totalitarian police state.

Humanists tell us over and over again that in a "pluralistic" society, we Christians have no right to "legislate morality." That is a lie. Every law is based upon some moral principle. If there is to be any law at all, it must be founded upon *someone's* concept of right and wrong. Traditionally our legal system was established upon biblical principles. But today it is based upon what has been called "sociological law" not on the moral absolutes of the Bible, but on the whims and prejudices of liberal/humanist judges.

The Humanist Concept of *Pluralism* Is a Fraud

Until about fifty years ago, our society was solidly supported by a Judeo-Christian consensus. Generally speaking, we Americans had shared moral values, regardless of our religious or political beliefs (excluding Communism, of course). We agreed that killing unborn babies was murder, that prostitution was evil, that it was *perversion* for men to sodomize each other, that criminals were not the victims of society, but deserved to be punished for their actions. Because of our rich religious heritage, we knew that certain things were right and others were wrong.

But today millions of Americans have been brainwashed by the humanist media elite into believing that because we are a pluralistic nation, we are obliged to tolerate every form of antisocial, antichristian, antihuman behavior imaginable. We are not supposed to make "value judgments" or be condemnatory of the actions of rock star Ozzie Osborne when he bites off the heads of pigeons during his shows. After all, he is just "doing his own thing." We are labeled *bigots* and *narrow-minded* when we express shock when lesbian lovers attempt to adopt a child. We are ridiculed as *puritans* and *repressive* because we oppose mind-destroying drugs like marijuana, cocaine, and heroin.

The humanists have exploited the concept of pluralism in America by twisting it to serve their own perverted ends. But what will the future bring in America? You may not fully realize it, but you and I are in a battle against godless humanism. The humanists have bragged that they will convert America into a secular state by the year 2000. That means they have declared war on you, especially if you are a conservative, activist Christian. They will do everything in their power to close your Christian schools, censor your favorite TV evangelist, remove your church tax exemption—in short, drive the Christian church in America underground.

Get Involved in Fighting Humanism

In his foreword to *A Time for Anger,* Franky Schaeffer warned, "In the twentieth century, evangelical Christians in America have naively accepted the role assigned to us by an anti-religious, anti-Christian consensus in our society. We have been relegated to a cultural backwater, where we are meant to paddle around content in the knowledge that we are merely allowed to exist."[9]

But humanists will never be content to let us exist. They are going to destroy us and wipe the Christian church from the earth, if possible. We are a threat to their goal of creating a one-world dictatorship under their control.

Dr. Rousas J. Rushdoony observed, "The evangelical impact on American politics in 1980 and 1981 stirs up daily wrath in the press and from politicians, because it reintroduces into politics a dimension which politicians largely have sought to avoid: moral confrontation. The hatred for all such evangelical groups is not because of their real or fancied blunders but because they have reintroduced biblical morality into politics."[10]

In America we ultimately face a battle between the forces of godless humanism and Christianity. They cannot coexist unless Christianity is in control.

True Christianity and Christian thinking promotes liberty, freedom, and equality for all, within the bounds of law based on God's Word, the Bible. America has always been a prime example of such freedom within the law, until the last thirty years or so. Gradually we have seen the repressive measures of humanism exclude God, prayer, and the Bible from our tax-supported schools. It has removed religious traditions from our holidays; changed Easter vacation to spring break; curtailed the freedom of churches to expand in various communities; censored clean, wholesome books from our tax-supported libraries; forcibly taken children from parents who would impose moral restraints on their own offspring; and demanded that the state be permitted to counsel teenagers about their sexual practices, use of contraceptives, and abortion, *independent* of their parents and often contrary to the wishes of their parents. These are only some of the repressive antics of secular humanist thinking.

And remember, in the eighties they only control 65 percent of our government, 85 percent of our press, and 95 percent of our educational system. If we let them, by 1990 they will control 85 percent of our government, 95 percent of our press, and 100 percent of our educational system, within easy reach of their goal of 100 percent control by the year 2000. Then we will see just how much the humanists really believe in *pluralism, freedom,* and *liberty.* By then it will be too late!

Remember, Hitler, Mussolini, and Joseph Stalin were not Christians; they were humanists. As I have said in other books, all secular humanists are not Communists, but all Communists and socialists are humanists. Consequently, if secular humanism triumphs in America by the year 2000, we Christians will be fortunate to have the same freedoms now experienced by the citizens of Russia and China.

Now do you understand why Dr. Francis Schaeffer, Dr. Rousas J. Rushdoony, Dr. Jerry Falwell, Dr. Pat Robertson, Dr. James Kennedy, myself, and an increasing number of others are raising their voices in warning against the imminent dangers of a humanist takeover in this country?

This is no time for Christian neutrality! Jesus said, "You are either for me or against me." Secular humanism and everything it stands for opposes Jesus Christ. If you do not fight it with all your might, I predict it will have an irreversible effect on America by the year 1990.

Which Way, America?

America is being pulled in two directions: to the left by secular humanist thinkers and to the right by Christians and other believers in traditional moral values. All current surveys indicate that 84–90 percent of America's citizens want to live in a nation of laws with traditional moral values. A few thousand individuals in the media, government, education, and liberal organizations are actively pulling this country to the left. Many of them, sincere in trying to effect good for this country, cannot comprehend the chaos that lies ahead.

The other predominant influence in this pluralistic country is made up of many shades of moral and divine commitment. Unfortunately our media have dulled the seriousness of the situation to most of them. Only a few are aware of the dangers that await the next decade if humanist thinking prevails. If these few courageous souls succeed in awakening the millions of sleeping moralists, we can easily prevail in spite of the awesome power of our liberal dominated press. Our success will rest on two premises:

God is for us! Four times America has been pulled back from the brink of moral decadence through revivals like that of the Great Awakening in the 1740s. Millions of Christians are praying for great awakening number five—in the eighties. And that is a strong possibility. There are many growing signs of revival. Millions of Christians are beginning to pray for a mighty movement of the Spirit of God.

I predict that America will either experience a moral and spiritual revival in the eighties or humanism will gain a stranglehold on this country by the early nineties.

We outnumber the humanists fifty to one. However, we must first awaken the fifty to the dangerous ends of humanism's erroneous theories and then activate them to vote out of office all humanist thinkers without a commitment to moral values.

In a pluralistic society, we can well afford to let humanists live here as law abiding citizens. We cannot, however, permit them to pass our laws, educate our young, and interpret our news from their lib-

CONTRASTING IDEOLOGIES IN OUR PLURALISTIC SOCIETY

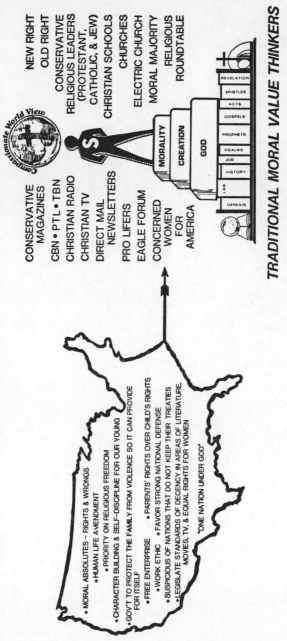

Compassionate World View

NEW RIGHT
OLD RIGHT
CONSERVATIVE RELIGIOUS LEADERS (PROTESTANT, CATHOLIC, & JEW)
CHRISTIAN SCHOOLS
CHURCHES
ELECTRIC CHURCH
MORAL MAJORITY
RELIGIOUS ROUNDTABLE

CONSERVATIVE MAGAZINES
CBN • PTL • TBN
CHRISTIAN RADIO
CHRISTIAN TV
DIRECT MAIL NEWSLETTERS
PRO LIFERS
EAGLE FORUM
CONCERNED WOMEN FOR AMERICA

REVELATION
EPISTLES
ACTS
GOSPELS
PROPHETS
PSALMS
JOB
HISTORY
LAW
GENESIS

MORALITY
CREATION
GOD

TRADITIONAL MORAL VALUE THINKERS

SOME GOV'T BUREAUCRATS • SOME JOURNALISTS
CONSERVATIVE POLITICAL ORGANIZATIONS
REPUBLICANS • DEMOCRATS • INDEPENDENTS
SUPPLY SIDE ECONOMISTS • MANY BUSINESSMEN
CONSERVATIVES • SOME EDUCATORS & JOURNALISTS

• MORAL ABSOLUTES - RIGHTS & WRONGS
• HUMAN LIFE AMENDMENT
• PRIORITY ON RELIGIOUS FREEDOM
• CHARACTER BUILDING & SELF-DISCIPLINE FOR OUR YOUNG
• GOV'T TO PROTECT THE FAMILY FROM VIOLENCE SO IT CAN PROVIDE FOR ITSELF
• FREE ENTERPRISE   • PARENTS' RIGHTS OVER CHILD'S RIGHTS
• WORK ETHIC   • FAVOR STRONG NATIONAL DEFENSE
• SUSPICIOUS OF NATIONS THAT DO NOT KEEP THEIR TREATIES
• LEGISLATE STANDARDS OF DECENCY IN AREAS OF LITERATURE, MOVIES, TV, & EQUAL RIGHTS FOR WOMEN
"ONE NATION UNDER GOD"

CONTRASTING IDEOLOGIES IN OUR PLURALISTIC SOCIETY

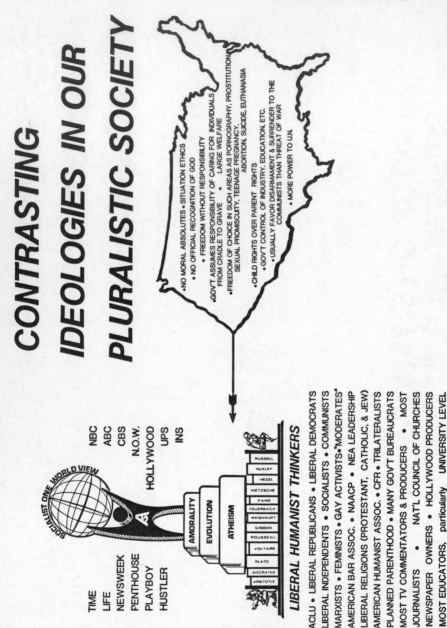

TIME
LIFE
NEWSWEEK
PENTHOUSE
PLAYBOY
HUSTLER

NBC
ABC
CBS
N.O.W.
HOLLYWOOD
UPS
INS

SOCIALIST ONE WORLD VIEW

AMORALITY
EVOLUTION
ATHEISM

RUSSELL
HUXLEY
HEGEL
NIETZSCHE
PAINE
FEUERBACH
WEISHAUPT
GIBBON
ROUSSEAU
VOLTAIRE
PLATO
SOCRATES
ARISTOTLE

- NO MORAL ABSOLUTES • SITUATION ETHICS
- NO OFFICIAL RECOGNITION OF GOD
- FREEDOM WITHOUT RESPONSIBILITY
- GOV'T ASSUMES RESPONSIBILITY OF CARING FOR INDIVIDUALS FROM CRADLE TO GRAVE • LARGE WELFARE
- FREEDOM OF CHOICE IN SUCH AREAS AS PORNOGRAPHY, PROSTITUTION, SEXUAL PROMISCUITY, TEENAGE PREGNANCY, ABORTION, SUICIDE, EUTHANASIA
- CHILD RIGHTS OVER PARENT RIGHTS
- GOV'T CONTROL OF INDUSTRY, EDUCATION, ETC.
- USUALLY FAVOR DISARMAMENT & SURRENDER TO THE COMMUNISTS THAN THREAT OF WAR
- MORE POWER TO U.N.

LIBERAL HUMANIST THINKERS

ACLU • LIBERAL REPUBLICANS • LIBERAL DEMOCRATS
LIBERAL INDEPENDENTS • SOCIALISTS • COMMUNISTS
MARXISTS • FEMINISTS • GAY ACTIVISTS • "MODERATES"
AMERICAN BAR ASSOC. • NAACP • NEA LEADERSHIP
LIBERAL RELIGIONS (PROTESTANT, CATHOLIC, & JEW)
AMERICAN HUMANIST ASSOC. • CFR • TRILATERALISTS
PLANNED PARENTHOOD • MANY GOV'T BUREAUCRATS
MOST TV COMMENTATORS & PRODUCERS •   MOST
JOURNALISTS   •   NAT'L COUNCIL OF CHURCHES
NEWSPAPER OWNERS • HOLLYWOOD PRODUCERS
MOST EDUCATORS, particularly UNIVERSITY LEVEL

eral/humanist perspective. Since we taxpayers pay the salaries of our government leaders, we have the traditional American right to vote them in or out of office. We owe it to our children and our children's children to put into office those who have a deep commitment to God, morality, and country.

5

Power of the Press

The concept of a free press in America is presently a myth. Let me explain what I mean.

Over 20,000 print publications appear in America today, ranging from daily newspapers to quarterly magazines and assorted journals. There are at least 1,700 daily papers and over 8,000 weeklies. In addition, the media include more than 8,900 radio stations and over 1,000 television stations. Of these TV stations, only 150 are independent (without any major network affiliation).[1]

All of these media sources convey information to the public around the clock, a veritable deluge of information—so much that it's bewildering to figure out what to absorb and what to ignore. Worse yet, however, it is almost impossible to ascertain what is true and what is given a liberal twist.

In America we have only the *appearance* of a free press. In our major news outlets, the liberal/humanists alone can freely express their views. The conservative/Christian viewpoint is usually distorted, ridiculed, or ignored, censored by men and women in the media who set forth a predetermined amoral outlook on life, a prescriptive world view they wish to foist upon the rest of us. They have limitless freedom of the press, whereas the majority in this country—the moral, the conservatives, and Christians—are denied that freedom.

As I have noted in earlier chapters, a small elitist group of liberal/humanists have seized monopolistic control of our major communications media and are using those outlets to brainwash the majority of decent Americans into accepting a one-world, godless view of life.

Before I continue with this theme, it might be beneficial to review some of the past history of the press in America in order to determine how we arrived at our present state.

The Press in Early America

The first newspaper in the thirteen colonies was Benjamin Harris's *Publick Occurrences, Both Forreign and Domestick,* published in Boston in September, 1690. It was going to be a monthly publication, but its first issue also turned out to be its last. Because Harris had not obtained a license required by law, Increase and Cotton Mather shut down his paper.

In those days the printing press was viewed by many government officials as a subversive weapon. Indeed, in Europe the invention of the printing press had been both a blessing and a curse, depending upon who controlled it. The same invention that had made the Bible widely available to the common man for the first time was also exploited by radicals, humanists, and pornographers.

During the years prior to the Revolutionary War, a free press in the colonies did not exist. And any printer who dared to exercise what he viewed as freedom of expression had to accept the consequences—whether from the government or from angry mobs. Yet, by the end of 1765, all but two of the colonies had newspapers—a total of twenty-three papers, all weeklies.

According to historian Frank Luther Mott, in his book, *American Journalism,* it was the passage of the British Stamp Act that started rumblings in the colonies against being ruled by the mother country. The Stamp Act, passed in 1765, required the use of specially stamped paper for all written or printed materials. The tax would have doubled the cost of printing newspapers. As a consequence, many folded. Still others simply continued to print on unstamped papers. There was such overall rebellion against the act that Parliament finally repealed the law.[2]

But this was the beginning of a rebellion that would culminate in the Revolutionary War and the birth of the United States of America.

Freedom of the press was early recognized by our Founding Fathers as an essential element if America was to be a strong and free nation. Thus a guarantee of such freedom was included in the First Amendment to the Constitution. This Amendment states, "Congress shall make no law respecting an establishment of religion, or prohibiting the free exercise thereof; or abridging the freedom of speech, or of the press; or the right of people peaceably to assemble, and to petition the Government for a redress of grievances."[3]

The Penny Papers

Until the 1830s, most American papers were printed mainly for the well educated. But in 1833 Benjamin Day founded the New York *Sun* and began selling it on the streets for a penny a copy. Two years later, James Gordon Bennett founded the New York *Morning Herald* as a competitor to the *Sun.*[4]

The penny papers brought about a change in the reporter's view. The traditional view was to report anything that was new. Simple enough. But as these newspapers competed with each other for sales and advertising dollars, the whole concept of "news" changed. Reporters were less concerned with reporting new events than selling newspapers.

According to Frank Luther Mott, there were three elements in this shift away from reporting straight news to reporting what would sell papers: an increase of local or home city news; much greater emphasis on sensational news, crime, and sex; and the appearance of what was later called human-interest news—stories of people who are interesting as human beings.[5]

Yellow Journalism

One of the first men to set up a journalistic empire was Hungarian-born Joseph Pulitzer. Founder of the Saint Louis *Post-Dispatch,* he later moved to New York and bought the *World* in 1883. Pulitzer's papers were characterized by sensationalism, exploitation of crime and scandal, and social crusades.

William Randolph Hearst, son of a wealthy miner who struck it rich in the West, came to New York in 1895 and bought the *New York Journal* to compete with Pulitzer. The fierce competition between

Hearst and Pulitzer resulted in some obvious abuses of press free-dom—among them the fomenting of the Spanish-American War. According to historian Mott:

> There seems to be a great probability in the frequently reiterated statement that if Hearst had not challenged Pulitzer to a circulation contest at the time of the Cuban insurrection, there would have been no Spanish-American War. Certainly the most powerful and persistent jingo propaganda ever carried on by newspapers was led by the New York *Journal* and *World* in 1896–98, and the result was an irresistible popular fervor for war which at length overcame the long unwillingness of President McKinley and even swept blindly over the last-minute capitulation of Spain on all the points at issue.[6]

Hearst had purchased a yacht, the *Vamoose,* in 1897 and had sent it to Cuba with writer Richard Harding Davis and Frederick Remington, a famous illustrator, aboard. Remington, disliking his assignment, wished to return home. In a classic telegram exchange between Remington and Hearst, Remington said, "Everything is quiet. There is no trouble here. There will be no war. Wish to return." To which Hearst responded, "Please remain. You furnish the pictures, I'll furnish the war."[7]

Although the Spanish-American War lasted no longer than three months, over 4,000 Americans died, but Hearst and Pulitzer had sold millions of newspapers. They had clearly shown the power of the press—when exercised irresponsibly.

The *New York Times*

In his book, *The Elite Press,* journalist John C. Merrill describes the place of the *New York Times* in American life. The *Times,* explains Merrill, is one of the elite newspapers of the world. By *elite* Merrill means newspapers that have an international outlook—rejecting such outmoded ideas as patriotism and nationalism.[8]

Elite newspapers are those that cater "to the intelligentsia and the opinion leaders. . . ." They are papers concerned more with ideas and interpretation than with the reporting of human events. According to

Merrill, ". . . It is this press that people who desire to be informed or indoctrinated with the 'line,' will want to read regularly."[9]

Although the circulation of elite newspapers may be small, they are avidly read by the liberal/humanist elitists in America—public officials, scholars, journalists, theologians, lawyers, judges, and business leaders. The *Times* has readers in every state in the union and in nearly 85 percent of all counties in the fifty states. You will find it on microfilm in more than 2,000 libraries across America, and the *Times* biography service provides a monthly collection of obituaries and human interest features on public figures.

In addition the New York Times Company offers a news feature service, owns a paper company, Arno Press, Times Books, broadcasting companies, and twenty-one newspapers. It has holdings in Canada, England, France, Australia, and New Zealand.

Its influence on the communications media and other opinion leaders in America is alarming. Many newsmen, editors, and commentators at the major networks take their news and editorial cues from the *Times*. Unfortunately, the editorial policies of the *Times* determine what news is printed—and what is ignored altogether.

That editorial policy admittedly promotes a one-world socialist viewpoint.

The nuclear freeze movement would be dead without the *New York Times* and the other papers it influences. On March 20, 1983, the *Times* gave three columns, including pictures, to six freeze protesters who were arrested for lying down on the street in front of the Vandenberg missile site. In a free society I can understand coverage of six people willing to go to jail for breaking the law to communicate their convictions, but I can't understand why a newspaper doesn't consider 300,000 people gathered in Washington, D.C., for prayer (the second largest crowd in the District of Columbia's history) sufficiently newsworthy to rate any mention at all. Could it be that the paper which proclaims that it prints "all the news that's fit to print" considers six protesters more important than 300,000 prayers?

Another possibility, of course, is that the nuclear-freeze movement would help to make us inferior in strength to Russia and thus would help to advance internationalist ideology. Advertising the fact that

300,000 prayer warriors want to pray this nation back to moral sanity would not.

New York Times editor and key establishment spokesman James Reston believes that all journalists should be internationalists. In his book, *The Artillery of the Press,* Reston affirms that "... the rising power of the United States in world affairs ... requires not a more compliant press, but a relentless barrage of facts and criticism, as noisy but also as accurate as artillery fire. This means a less provincial, even a less nationalistic press."[10]

The *New York Times,* of course, has been leftist and internationalist since Adolph Ochs received financing from international bankers to purchase the paper in 1896.

Adolph Ochs began his publishing career as a typesetter on the *Louisville Courier Journal.* At the age of twenty, he managed to purchase a failing paper, the Chattanooga *Times,* in 1878. When he was thirty-eight, he decided it was time to leave Tennessee and move to New York City. Apparently he intended to purchase the *New York Mercury,* but the deal fell through. When he discovered that the *New York Times* was having financial problems, he decided to buy it.

Leonard and Mark Silk explain what happened when Ochs approached the men who controlled the paper. "Ochs impressed the financiers Charles R. Flint, General Sam Thomas, J. P. Morgan and August Belmont, who controlled the paper, as a smart newspaperman who might save their investment."[11] What Leonard and Mark Silk fail to mention is that these backers were international bankers with financial interests in America and Europe, interested in gaining control of our communications media in America. It was—and still is—the goal of the internationalists to manipulate public opinion in favor of a one-world government.

These internationalists were simply following a plan laid out by British industrialist Cecil Rhodes for the subjugation of the world under British rule. Rhodes had formed a secret society and various front groups throughout the English-speaking world to carry out this objective. In the deepest levels of his secret society were a group of wealthly financiers known as the Circle of Initiates. An outer circle was called the Association of Helpers. This outer ring was later renamed the Round Table Organization.

According to Dr. Carroll Quigley, it soon became apparent to Rhodes and his fellow conspirators that additional front organizations were needed to push for this one-world government under British rule. One of these front organizations was called the Royal Institute of International Affairs. "In New York, it was known as the Council of Foreign Relations, and was a front for J. P. Morgan and Company."[12]

It is interesting to note that Adolph Ochs was an early member of the Council on Foreign Relations and that control of the *New York Times* has *always* remained in the hands of CFR members: Adolph Ochs, Arthur Hays Sulzberger, Orvil E. Dryfoos, and the current head of the *Times* empire, Arthur Ochs Sulzberger.

Because of its immense influence in our communications media, the *Times* has done untold damage to our nation and to the free world.

The Wire Services and Biased Reporting

Several years ago, on one of my speaking tours around the country, I learned a profitable lesson about the awesome power of the media monopolists.

Before catching my plane in Atlanta, Georgia, I picked up a copy of the *Atlanta Constitution*. In Washington, D.C., I bought the *Washington Post* and the *New York Times* as well. On my return trip to Los Angeles, I purchased a copy of the *Los Angeles Times*. To my amazement, these four influential newspapers carried the *same* articles on their front pages.

At that point I was struck by the awesome power of the press in influencing the way we think about the world around us. Here were newspapers from different parts of the country, all saying the same thing to their readers. It made me realize the tremendous responsibility of wire-service reporters. Their news stories are not just published in one city newspaper, but distributed by wire to thousands of daily newspapers and thousands of radio and television stations as well. Just think of the power wielded by *one* wire service reporter. A liberal/humanist reporter can reach *millions* of Americans every day, to shape public opinion.

Both the Associated Press and United Press International have histories of leftist biases. Indeed, their prejudices were obvious in the 1960 presidential race between John Kennedy and Richard Nixon.

Richard F. Pourade, editor emeritus of the *San Diego Union,* was so alarmed at the distortions being printed during the campaign that he did a detailed study of the slanted reporting. He reported some of his findings in *Human Events,* beginning with these words: "The coverage of the 1960 political campaign by the Associated Press and United Press International indicates that interpretative writing has opened a new and disturbing era of personal journalism."[13]

The wire-service reporters, charged Pourade, were more interested in writing their own opinions about what they *thought* was happening during the campaign than they were in reporting straight news. As he observed, "In story after story, the reporters read motives into the words and actions of the candidates and, upon occasion, imputed base political motives to positions and statements."[14]

"Wire service reporters," noted Pourade, "set themselves up as a final judge of crowds, reactions, sincerity of statement, pertinency of the statements politically and ideologically, and passed judgment on the merits of various proposals. Too often, what the candidate had to say was buried beneath how the reporter personally evaluated it in the context of the whole campaign, and what he thought was the crowd's reaction to it."[15]

Pourade continued, "There isn't any doubt that what the candidates said and what they did was measured by the personal ideology of the reporter. It is good or bad depending upon what the reporter believes. As a result, personal feelings have permeated the entire UPI and AP copy. It suggests a serious lack of proper control in editing."[16]

Biased reporting—such as that normally found in AP and UPI dispatches—can make or break a political candidate. In this case, the liberal reporters desperately wanted John Kennedy elected president, so they slanted their articles in such a way as to discredit Nixon and laud Kennedy. They conducted an effective campaign against Senator Barry Goldwater in 1964 and did everything they could to get Jimmy Carter elected in 1976.

A biased or inaccurate report sent out over a wire service can do irreparable damage to nations as well. The report will be duplicated thousands of times in newspapers, radio, and television. Once the damage has been done, a retraction or correction profits little.

El Salvador Misinformation

Reed Irvine, editor of the *AIM Report,* recently illustrated how irresponsible journalism can damage the future stability of a nation.

On March 15, 1983, UPI correspondent John Newhagen filed a report from El Salvador, which began "The American Embassy said in a report released Tuesday that $25 million in U.S. loans to El Salvador's land reform program have disappeared and recommended the funds be written off as a loss. . . . Opposition parties have charged the Agrarian Reform Institute was rife with corruption."[17]

Newhagen's report came at a time when the White House was urging Congress to approve additional funds to help El Salvador fight the Communist terrorists and weakened Reagan's position. As a result of Newhagen's report, Charles Osgood of the CBS Radio Network picked up the story and elaborated on it in a report on March 16.

As it turns out, *the dispatch was inaccurate.* Reed Irvine comments, "The $25 million mentioned in the consultant's report was not missing and it was not money lent or guaranteed by the U.S. Government. It represented the unpaid portion of loans made by the Salvadoran government from its own resources in the early days of the agrarian reform program. Of the total, only the local currency equivalent of about $200,000 could not be accounted for."[18]

The UPI put out a correction on the Newhagen dispatch March 18, but the damage was already done. One man—a wire-service reporter—can spread a mistaken report across America and actually threaten the future survival of a nation!

UPI Changes Ownership

United Press International, owned by the E. W. Scripps Company since 1897, has been sold to Media News, based in Nashville, Tennessee. Media News was formed by four men: Len R. Small, Cordell J. Overgaard, Douglas F. Ruhe, and William E. Geisler. Since Media News purchased UPI in 1982, another partner has joined this group:

John Jay Hooker. In January of 1983, Hooker bought one-third interest in UPI. According to reporter Wendell Rawls, Jr., writing in the *New York Times,* "Mr. Hooker is flamboyant and often a subject of publicity. He assisted and supported both John and Robert Kennedy. His political hero was Hubert H. Humphrey."[19]

The Associated Press

The Associated Press was formed in 1848 and has been the frontrunner of all the wire services in America. Keith Fuller is currently president, chief executive officer, and general manager of AP. Fuller, along with several board members, belongs to the Council on Foreign Relations.

The Frightening Elitists

Free access to diverse opinions evidences the strength of a democracy. How diverse can American elitist opinion be, when its media are tightly controlled by fewer than twelve people? If you think that is preposterous, just consider the fact that two major wire services, AP and UPI, serve thousands of our daily papers, and three TV networks—ABC, CBS, and NBC—control the news reporting and programming. In addition, we have a handful of major newspapers: the *New York Times, Washington Post, Los Angeles Times* (plus their many affiliate papers), magazines like *Time* (and its *Time/Life* affiliates) and *Newsweek* (owned by the owner of the *Washington Post*). Recently a new national newspaper has taken the country by storm, *USA Today,* owned and operated by the Gannett Newspaper Company. A reading of this very interesting paper would indicate to me that it shares the same liberal/humanist commitment as the others.

It is frightening to realize that these ten corporations provide the news information sources for most of our nation's citizens. The ideology of these organizations is controlled by the ten people at the head, who will determine the standard of moral values to be advocated in all media. (It would be interesting to see if any conservatives are employed by these corporate heads.) Even more frightening, most of these corporate heads are members of the Council on Foreign Relations, an organization committed to establishing an internationalist order, which, of course, they hope to control.

Liberals/Humanists Hate Conservative Christians

Have you ever noticed how "tolerant" liberal/humanists are? One can be anything he wants to be—a homosexual, a transsexual, a drug pusher, a feminist—anything but a conservative or Christian. If he takes an aggressive stand for the free enterprise system, Judeo-Christian morality, or a strong national defense, watch out. The liberals/humanists will do everything they can to destroy him.

There are two reasons why they hate conservatives and Christians. One is because they regard us as a threat to their dominant control of our culture. They realize that we represent commitment and that our churches, Christian schools and colleges, publishing companies, and communication outlets can potentially awaken enough citizens to throw off the yoke of oppression they would impose on us. Humanists can only retain control of a country if they can censor the information, education, and communication industries. Humanism, like Communism, thrives on the ignorance of the masses, who must be controlled by the leftists. Conservatives and Christians are a threat to that control, and they know it.

The other reason that humanists hate us is because they have no biblically based moral values. Situation ethics and pragmatism shape their whole world view. They make up their morality to fit their circumstances, invariably looking to government to solve all social problems. We have already seen that they are usually internationalists, dedicated to some vague notion of "world peace" through a new world order.

And because of their godless view of life, they are more inclined to agree philosophically with socialists and Communists on political and moral issues than with conservative Christians. To their way of thinking the only real enemy is anyone who believes in God and is committed to traditional moral values.

Although they will do their best to unearth scandal in the lives of prominent conservatives and Christians, they offer a different standard for their liberal/humanist allies in government. If a scandal comes to light that might ruin the career of some immoral collectivist, these liberal/humanist reporters will minimize the crime. They will either ignore it altogether or bury the story in the middle of the paper, where no one will notice. You see, they are concerned more about keeping their own kind in power than in telling the truth.

Like a pro-football line defending its quarterback, the hidden censors of the media protect the American people from truth, morality, and absolute forms of information. Instead of opening the door to freedom, they slant the news and filter the truth wherever possible, distorting the words, actions, and interests of all with whom they disagree. Media censorship is called "news management." They ignore what they do not consider newsworthy and distort what they cannot ignore.

Someone asked me why our Congress, state governments, and many local governments are more liberal than the presidency. I replied that the media can ignore congressional and local candidates with whom they disagree, but a presidential candidate cannot be sidestepped or stifled. That is why many congressmen and senators are far more liberal than their constituents. It is very difficult for a traditional American to compete against a liberal-backed and equally liberal press. Their favored candidate can do no wrong, for if he makes a mistake, it is omitted or explained away; if the conservative stumbles, it hits page one.

Reagan triumphs regardless of the press. In 1980, despite hatred, distortion, and obvious disapproval, the press could not keep American people from electing the one conservative candidate the liberals and humanists had intended to defeat.

The great conservative landslide victory in the election of 1980 provides a classic illustration. During the primaries, 320 of the leading newspaper editors and reporters met in Washington, D.C. A straw poll was taken to see whom they favored for president of the United States. The following chart reflects the results:

109	John Anderson
60	Ted Kennedy
57	President Jimmy Carter

HUMANISTIC IN PHILOSOPHY

31	George Bush	HUMANISTIC MODERATES
24	Howard Baker	
20	Ronald Reagan	CONSERVATIVE

Media's Influence May Destroy Public Figures

Barry Goldwater. In 1964 Senator Barry Goldwater learned some bitter lessons about the press. He was victimized by a hostile news media and nearly destroyed politically by the Johnson administration's cleverly contrived hate propaganda, which portrayed him as a madman determined to blow up the world.

Do you recall that thirty-second commercial aimed against Goldwater? It showed a little girl in the middle of a beautiful field, picking petals from a flower. Then we saw a hand reaching for a hot button at the White Hosue and the girl engulfed in a hydrogen bomb explosion. Following that appeared a picture of Goldwater. An announcer asked the grim question, "Do you want his hand on the button?"

Goldwater's treatment by the liberal press was no better. Goldwater says, "I yield to no other American politican for the dubious distinction of being a political candidate whose image was totally distorted by the television news media."[20]

Goldwater wonders why every American in public life must be required to get the approval of a "group of individuals whose only assignment and whose only job is to record and recite the news. Nobody has endowed Mr. Huntley, Mr. Brinkley, Mr. Reynolds or any of the other network TV commentators with special powers. My feeling has long been that Mr. Brinkley's opinion is about as important as that held by the boy who brings you your evening newspaper."[21]

Nixon and Watergate. When the liberal press got wind of the Watergate break-in, it was just the sort of scandal they needed to drive Nixon from office. Nixon and the press had been at odds for years.

Conservative political analyst Victor Lasky has written a fascinating book on the Watergate scandal called *It Didn't Start With Watergate.* In it, he observes that Watergate was purely a "media event."[22] It was

LIBERALS DOMINATE THE MEDIA

Liberal   *Conservative*
0   50   100

Political personalities

DAVID ROCKEFELLER	JOHN F. KENNEDY		JIMMY CARTER	GERALD FORD	RICHARD NIXON		RONALD REAGAN	
JERRY BROWN	ALAN CRANSTON	LYNDON JOHNSON	JOHN GLENN	GEORGE BUSH			PHIL CRANE	JESSE HELMS
FRANK CHURCH	BIRCH BAYH					BARRY GOLDWATER		JACK KEMP
GEORGE McGOVERN	JESSE JACKSON		HENRY KISSINGER					BILL ARMSTRONG
	WALTER MONDALE							JEREMIAH DENTON

Media personalities

EDWARD R. MURROW

WALTER CRONKITE   CHET HUNTLEY

ERIC SEVAREID   HARRY REASONER

DAN RATHER   DAVID BRINKLEY

MIKE WALLACE   BRIAN GUMBEL   TED KOPPEL

BARBARA WALTERS   TOM BROKAW   JANE PAULEY

HOWARD K. SMITH   DANIEL SCHORR
ROGER MUDD

SAM DONALDSON

MARVIN KALB

Media vehicles

ATLANTA CONSTITUTION   TIME LIFE   CNN

WASHINGTON POST   NEWSWEEK

NBC   PBS   U.S. NEWS & WORLD REPORT

CBS

ABC

NEW YORK TIMES

LOS ANGELES TIMES

a burglary blown all out of proportion by a media elite determined to destroy Richard Nixon at all costs.

Lasky's book is a serious indictment of the leftist media elite—an elite that conveniently overlooked far worse crimes perpetrated by Franklin Roosevelt, John Kennedy, and Lyndon Johnson. Crimes of wiretapping, sexual immorality, drug abuse, all these and more were swept under the rug to protect these liberal presidents from destruction. Had our liberal press been as concerned about publishing the truth about these presidents as in trying to destroy conservatives and Christians, all three of them would have been humiliated and driven from office.

For example, at the time John Kennedy was president, the current executive editor of the *Washington Post,* Ben Bradlee, was Washington Bureau chief for *Newsweek* magazine. Bradlee and Kennedy were good friends and met frequently. In 1975 Bradlee published *Conversations with Kennedy,* a book that reveals how morally depraved Kennedy was. Bradlee admits that Kennedy asked him about the possibility of digging up dirt on his political adversaries and publishing them. Wiretapping, prying into tax returns of opponents, election fraud, misuse of federal agencies—all of these practices were used or discussed by Kennedy.

According to Lasky, Kennedy was also a notorious womanizer. He had carried on numerous affairs, including romances with Marilyn Monroe and mafia associate Judith Campbell Exner.

As a journalist supposedly dedicated to printing the "truth," where was Bradlee's concern for "truth" in dealing with Kennedy? He knew Kennedy was living a lie, cheating on his wife, and breaking the law. Yet Bradlee said nothing until years later.

Lyndon Johnson was also protected from exposure by the liberal media. He had authorized wiretaps on Martin Luther King and Robert Kennedy. He was fascinated to learn of King's extramarital affairs, all of which were dutifully recorded by FBI agents as King traveled throughout the country preaching peace and love. Johnson had passed these tapes around to his friends and the press corps knew of their existence. Yet they did nothing.

Later the liberal press turned on Johnson after the Gulf of Tonkin Resolution was passed by Congress on August 7, 1964. It was their continual harassment against him that kept him from running for a second term of office.

Jerry Falwell. Just contrast the coverups by the press of corruption in the Kennedy and Johnson administrations with the destructive barrages leveled against men like Jerry Falwell and former Secretary of the Interior James Watt.

Jerry Falwell, one of America's most respected ministers of the Gospel, has been characterized by the American news media as a reincarnated Hitler, a Jim Jones cultist, an Ayatollah of the Religious Right, and a man who would close down every library in America and plunge America into the Dark Ages.

Why do they hate and fear Falwell so much? He has never assaulted anyone. He has never slandered or cheated anyone. Yet the media are so powerful that they have almost convinced our citizens that he will establish a "right wing" dictatorship in America. Jerry Falwell's crime is that he favors laws to protect the lives of unborn children; he wants to permit children to pray in school; he wants to keep drugs and pornography from polluting the minds of teenagers and adults.

Here is a typical example of the deliberate distortion of the press. The January 10, 1983, issue of *People* magazine printed an article written by Gery Clifford. The headline read, "His Critics Speak Out and Jerry Falwell's Home Base Becomes a Flock Divided."

The headline itself was blatantly inaccurate. It gave the impression that Falwell's church congregation was violently split over his pro-moral activities in America. But that's not the case at all. I have preached in Jerry's church four times to capacity crowds. If that's division, I pray God will send it to every congregation in America! Gery Clifford claims to have interviewed three "prominent" ministers in Lynchburg who were critical of Falwell. In actuality, two of the ministers don't even have churches in Lynchburg, and not one of them would be known by more than a handful of people in the community.

The article then goes on to charge that Jerry Falwell is the owner of a shopping mall that contains a bar. Not only that, he is unwilling to pay taxes on "his" mall. The truth is that Jerry Falwell himself owns no shopping mall. Years ago his ministry, the Old Time Gospel Hour, rented a building in the mall for office space. In 1980 the owner of the mall offered to sell it to the ministry. The Old Time Gospel Hour purchased the mall, along with its tax-paying current tenants—including a grocery store and restaurant which sell alcoholic beverages. As the leases on these stores run out, the ministry will move its operation into the vacant stores. The tax issue (a court case) has nothing whatsoever to do with the mall, but concerns Liberty Baptist College property, miles away.

But the impression is left in the reader's mind that Falwell's community is in an uproar over his activities, that he owns a bar, and that he is a tax rebel to boot!

Such obvious media distortions are commonplace. It must have infuriated the liberal/humanist reporters no end when *Good Housekeeping* magazine, in early 1983, published the results of its "Most Admired Men Poll."[23] This poll showed that *Good Housekeeping* readers chose Ronald Reagan as the most admired man in the nation, followed by Jerry Falwell and Billy Graham. Once again, the media elite are totally out of step with the majority of the people in the United States.

James Watt.   Former Secretary of the Interior James Watt has been another victim of media bias and scorn. Together with left-wing environmental groups, the media elite portrayed James Watt as a Bible-toting lunatic determined to destroy America's wilderness areas with strip mines, parking lots, oil refineries, and fast-food restaurants.

From reading press reports and listening to wild-eyed radical environmentalists, you would imagine that James Watt was a madman. But the truth is that he's a devout Christian who is firmly committed to the preservation of America's wilderness areas.

During his tour in Washington he learned to deal with the press. In an interview in *Charisma* magazine, Watt observed, ". . . Most of the Washington press corps is unreliable. If you don't expect any more from them than performing at their level to destroy and ridicule and create conflict, then they are performing as you expect them to and you shrug your shoulders and move on."[24]

In February of 1983, James Watt delivered a speech to fifty of his employees at the Beverly Hilton in Beverly Hills. In his talk, he pointedly remarked that the press had badly distorted his position on nearly every environmental issue.

Media critics have blamed Watt for the decline in the purchase of new parklands. But it was not Watt who introduced the concept of reducing funding for new lands. According to Watt, "Every one of my critics in the congressional delegation from California voted to cut funds for acquiring parklands in America and I want that understood." The amount of money Congress has appropriated for the purchase of parklands steadily declined from $386.9 million in 1978 to $102.7 million in 1981. The 1982 appropriation totalled only $71.2 million.

Critics have also failed to give him proper credit for his efforts to maintain and restore the parklands already owned by the government. "The first year I came into office," stated Watt, "I asked Congress to double the amount of money available to the national park system, to more than double it."[25]

Watt has also been repeatedly attacked for supposedly wanting to open up wilderness areas to mineral, oil, and gas exploration. That's a media lie, too. "We will not be mining or drilling for oil and natural gas in the national parks. . . . We are talking about those multiple-use lands that Congress said should be managed for their multiple-use benefits."[26]

According to Watt, some 340 million acres have been set aside as multiple-use lands. If utilized properly, these lands "will yield 85 percent of all the domestic oil and gas to be found in the United States." Two-thirds of these valuable resources will be located in offshore oil and gas leases. Offshore oil production has declined from 725 million barrels per year in 1971 to approximately 425 million barrels in 1982. This alarms Watt. "We've got to see that this is reversed if we are going to take care of our military and our consumer interests and take care of the environment."[27]

Contrary to the image of Watt presented in the news media, he is a mild-mannered man who viewed his position as secretary of the interior as one of servanthood. The flack generated by the press made him more aware than ever of the need for Christians to get involved in politics.

If America is to be turned around, those who are committed to the fundamental principles of the Judeo-Christian ethic must get involved in politics. We were raised that if you wanted to be socially accepted, you didn't talk about politics or religion. That is wrong on both counts. As a consequence, many good people in America did not get involved in politics and did not discuss religion.

The consequence is a vacuum in the positions of leadership. Those who were not committed to the fundamentals of the Judeo-Christian community took over, and humanistic forces came on America.

Now we talk about our problems being drugs, alcoholism, abortion and school prayer. Those aren't the problems, but the symptoms. If the American people in the Christian community get involved in politics and discuss politics and religion and their role, there will be a chance of recovery. But will they? I'm not sure.[28]

This is the man who was finally driven from his post by a combination of hostile reporters, radical environmentalists, and liberal congressmen. Watt reluctantly resigned as secretary of the interior on October 9, 1983. After suffering public ridicule for two and a half years at the hands of a biased, anticonservative, antichristian press, James Watt could endure no more.

Unfortunately, he is not going to be the last public figure to be mercilessly taunted by a powerful news media. The left-leaning reporters will soon find another scapegoat to heap their ridicule upon. They will continue to distort and confuse the important issues of the day to suit their own interests.

They will continue to attack men like James Watt as symbols of the conservative Christianity they hate. It would be appropriate to conclude this section with a comment by Barry Goldwater: ". . . The press, the radio and television stand indicted of the crime of failing in their great and growing responsibility to give the American people an honest picture of the news of the day."[29] It was true when Goldwater was being victimized, and it is still true today.

Media Bigotry in Grenada Invasion Coverage

The United States invasion of the Communist-controlled Caribbean Island of Grenada offers an excellent illustration of the pro-Communist bigotry of the media.

First, liberal television newscasters criticized the president for sending in the marines to protect the lives of 1,000 United States medical students at the university. They sanctimoniously acted as though he was infringing on the legally constituted government of Grenada. The truth was, in 1979, the dedicated Communist dictator Bishop had taken over the tiny island by force from the local police with the backing of Communist Cuba. He didn't prove cooperative enough with them in their plans to foment Communist rebellion throughout the other islands. They arranged a revolution to replace him with a more militant Communist dictator who would impose Communism on those defenseless islands.

Special newscasts suddenly popped up on TV and radio featuring interviews of leftist senators and congressmen whose soft-on-Communism voting record showed their naiveté on Communist aggression. Not once did I see a conservative legislator given the opportunity of defending the action of the president. And even when a private citizen interviewed turned out to be pro-American, it was followed by some leftist Communist.

However, plenty of time was given the Grenada Ambassador to the United Nations to condemn the president for his "aggressive action." But no mention was made that the man was appointed by a committed Communist dictator who does not believe in "bipartisanship" or "pluralism." You can be sure the UN Ambassador he appointed was as committed to Communist control of the Caribbean as the dictator who appointed him. Besides, who cares what the Communists think of our president? And who cares if the murderous gangster, Yuri Andropov, condemns his actions in Grenada. Andropov's troops are still in Afghanistan.

The newspapers were scarcely better. The day after the marines landed and restored freedom to the inhabitants of Grenada for the first time in five years, the front page of many leftist newspapers carried the pictures of Communists in Havana raising their clenched fists in opposition to the United States action. Who cares what the Communists think? Certainly not the 100,000 freedom-loving Grenadians, or the citizens of nearby Barbados, or the other islands who were being threatened by a Communist takeover. Why didn't our left-leaning censors of the media ask the thousands of political prisoners of Cuba who opposed the Communist takeover of their country what they thought about it? Because they don't want the American people to realize what a costly mistake it was in 1962 when our leftist president, John Kennedy, refused to send the marines into Cuba to restore freedom on that tiny island just ninety miles south of Florida.

The hidden censors of our media, including the TV networks, liberal radio stations, and much of our leftist press, seldom moan when Communists like Dr. Fidel Castro, General Jaruzelski, Joseph Mugabe, Ho Chi Minh, or the Nicaraguan dictator cruelly murder their own countrymen to maintain their Communist control over the lives of millions of unfortunate souls. But let President Reagan, General Westmoreland, or the marines in Grenada strike a blow for freedom, and the censors go to work on them with their vicious suggestions that they are warmongers.

If Communism ever triumphs over the United States, I am inclined to believe that many in the media will welcome them and go right on doing what they do best—twisting the news to put Communism in the best possible light.

In the meantime, if enough people become aware of their leftist leanings, the real intentions of our hidden censors of the media will not be so hidden. And all it takes for good people to triumph is for enough good people to be confronted with the truth.

Distortions in *The Day After* and *Kennedy*

ABC recently demonstrated its left-wing bias in a $7 million fiasco called *The Day After,* a not-so-subtle attempt by the network to use "the federally controlled airwaves" to scare the American people into urging our leaders to throw down their arms and welcome the butchers from Moscow, rather than face the *possibility* of a nuclear explosion.

They seem to have forgotten the words of former President Franklin D. Roosevelt who said, "The only thing we have to fear is fear itself."

Such biased use of the television airwaves is a gross miscarriage of justice and indicates that the hidden censors know they are so powerful they really don't have to remain hidden anymore.

NBC at the same time produced their incredibly distorted docurama, *Kennedy*, which was thoroughly investigated for inaccuracies by Reed Irvine of Accuracy in Media. Targeted for a smear job in this "docudrama" was the late FBI director, J. Edgar Hoover. Hoover is presented as a crook, liar, homosexual, blackmailer, mama's boy, racist, paranoid, and misogynist.

Hoover was also presented as a lifelong antagonist of Kennedy's father, Joseph. In the movie, Joseph Kennedy warns his son John about Hoover in these words, "You better be careful, Jack. Hoover will try and wreck everything. He's not only a crook, he's a fag. And he knows a lot about us, Jack. He's made that his business."

The impression is clearly given that Hoover and Joseph Kennedy were lifelong enemies, but that simply isn't so. Accuracy in Media reports that on the wall of Hoover's office, from 1955 until his death, was a warm letter from Joe Kennedy, thanking him for his friendship and proclaiming J. Edgar Hoover "... one of the two men in public life today for whose opinion I give one continental ... if you should ever appear on the ticket of either party, I would guarantee you the largest contribution you would ever get from anybody and the hardest work by either Democrat or Republican."

In discussing the incredible distortions of this movie, columnist Patrick Buchanan observed, "The national networks, news as well as entertainment divisions, seem to have become giant engines of destruction. Wired up to every home, they routinely undermine traditional values and beliefs, rip up historic reputations, tear down respected institutions—from the FBI to the CIA, from the armed forces to the business community."

The Day After and *Kennedy* are simply two more clear examples of the depths to which the hidden censors will go to push their particular liberal/humanist world view upon the rest of us.

Communists or Marxists?

One of the clever ruses of our media controllers is to substitute the word *Marxist* for *known Communists.* Evidently they think *Marxist* is a more acceptable term. It tends to emphasize the ideological and intellectual aspect of Communism, and they hopefully want us to think there is a difference. If Communism ever triumphs over America, they will surely murder most of the 69 million Christians in our country, along with other conservatives and many moderates. What difference does it make if the man who pulls the trigger is a Marxist or a Communist? And if you doubt the reality of that prediction, you should ask the relatives of those murdered after the Communist takeovers of Russia, Poland, China, Vietnam, Cambodia, Nicaragua, and Afghanistan. Don't ask the hidden censors of the media, because they can't or won't see the truth, even when it stares them in the face. They still want our leaders to sit down and "negotiate" with the murderers of the innocent victims of Korean flight 007. Until our media manipulators understand that murderers are not normal human beings, they are unfit to interpret the events of national security.

Media pundits and liberal politicians selected by them to evaluate current events repeatedly demand that our president sit down and negotiate with Yuri Andropov. How do you carry on a meaningful discussion with a murderer, who has no respect for human life? Until our media "experts" understand the nature of Communism, they are unfit to comment on foreign affairs over the federally controlled airways as though theirs was the only rational view of political action.

The Need for a Media Review Board

I first became aware of the immense power of the media—and the desperate need for a media review board—many years ago, when I was a young pastor in Minnesota. One of my church members, a man who had lost an arm in an accident, had overcome his handicap and been elected county tax assessor.

When he came up for reelection, nearly everyone expected an easy victory. He had performed well and gained the respect of the entire community. But then the local newspaper decided to publish an investigative report on his past performance. In big, front-page stories, the reporter claimed that with the help of aerial photographs, he had discovered 109 different properties in the county that had been ignored by the tax assessor. He clearly implied that this honest, hardworking man had been incompetent or worse in carrying out his duties.

As a result of this "investigative report," he lost the election, and his political career was destroyed. He had been humiliated and disgraced in his community. *Later,* as it turned out, it was proved beyond a shadow of a doubt that these 109 properties were such worthless structures as dilapidated sheds, lean-tos, and garages. Not one of them was tax worthy. When the paper discovered its "mistake," it published a small retraction and buried it in the back pages, where few people saw it. The damage was already done—irreparable damage to a man's reputation and political future.

The LA Times "Report"

I have had the same kind of experience with the press. When it became known that I was involved with the Moral Majority, a reporter who worked for the *Los Angeles Times* visited me. I felt instinctively that she planned to distort everything I said, but I consented to the interview anyway. I asked her point-blank during the interview, "Is this going to be a hatchet job?" She hotly protested, "I don't do hatchet jobs!"

I spent more than seven hours with her on numerous occasions, giving her every possible bit of information I could about my own church and the many ministries that had developed out of it. Frankly, I expected a positive report. Surely she would mention that our church membership had multiplied to ten times our original number in twenty-five years or that 2,500 children were getting a Christian education in our school system of ten schools, including two fully accredited high schools. I was naive enough to think she might comment on my founding of Christian Heritage College or that employment in our church had gone from 3 people in 1956 to 337 (in all our enterprises) when I resigned. None of that was mentioned.

When the article was printed, it turned out to be a hatchet job from beginning to end. When I asked the reporter what had happened, she explained that her first story had been rejected by the editor. He had shoved it back into her hand and insisted that she "put more acid in it." So she rewrote it—with the acid. The article ended up being an attack on my personal character.

It was bad enough to endure a broadside in a major newspaper, but what happened after the article was printed startled me. That article was clipped by the newspaper librarian and placed in my file at the *Times.* Thus whenever another reporter is seeking information, he will consult that file, read the unfair attack, and use biased material as the basis for still another article. In this fashion lies and distortions will be perpetuated endlessly. Of course, the effect of irresponsible reporting on a person's reputation is immaterial to the press—and the private citizen has little or no recourse.

Donald Wildmon Meets the Press

The arrogance and irresponsibility of the press still amazes me. I can recall a Washington, D.C., press conference in February of 1981. Donald Wildmon and Ron Godwin called it to announce the beginning of a clean-up TV campaign, sponsored by the Coalition for Better Television. Thirty-seven members of the press were there: representatives from the major TV networks, radio stations, newspapers, wire services, and magazines. As an observer, I cannot recall ever sitting in a more hostile environment.

After Don read his press release, the reporters jumped on him like wailing banshees. It was one of the most vicious attacks I have ever witnessed. In the accusatory questioning, their hatred and bias became clear to everyone. Almost every reporter was growling, "Who do you think you are to impose censorship on our 'free' media?"

At the same conference I noticed a *Washington Star* photographer standing near Phyllis Schlafly and my wife, Bev, Coalition Board members who spoke briefly in support of Don's campaign. He held his camera at waist level and kept taking pictures of the two women. I was curious as to why he was taking pictures at such an unusual angle. I discovered his purpose the next day when the *Star* published a photograph on the front page of Phyllis and Bev. The photographer had purposely shot them at a low angle to distort their features. The unflattering photograph made two good-looking women appear grotesque.

CBS Attacks General Westmoreland

One of the most blatant examples of liberal bias and irresponsibility was the documentary entitled *The Uncounted Enemy: A Vietnam Deception,* which aired over CBS on January 23, 1982.

In this supposedly honest investigation, Mike Wallace and his researchers tried their best to destroy the honor of General Westmoreland by charging him with covering up enemy troop figures during the Vietnam War.

As Westmoreland recently observed:

> I confess that I did not realize the seriousness of the victimization of people, of businesses and institutions by the powerful moguls of the

media until I myself became one of their victims. It is a frightening experience. The media can make false accusations that will be seen by millions of people. Skillful editing of videotapes can make these charges appear very convincing even when they are without the slightest foundation.[1]

The investigative reporters at CBS had begun with the basic assumption that Westmoreland was guilty, and they deliberately interviewed only people who would support their belief.

Immediately after the show aired, Westmoreland and his allies called a press conference to denounce the program as a fraud. Westmoreland has since filed a multimillion-dollar law suit against CBS for libeling him.

The documentary was so obviously biased that *TV Guide* reporters spent two months investigating how the show was researched and produced. They published a devastating indictment of CBS in their May 28, 1982 issue. "Anatomy of a Smear: How CBS News Broke the Rules and 'Got' Gen. Westmoreland," concludes with this comment: "The inaccuracies, distortions and violations of journalistic standards in 'The Uncounted Enemy' suggest that television news 'safeguards' for fairness and accuracy need tightening, if not wholesale revision."[2]

If *TV Guide* had not decided to investigate this documentary, we probably would never have known how CBS set out deliberately to smear Westmoreland. That is why I consider it so important that we establish a media review board to which people can bring their complaints when they have been maligned in the press. Far too many liberal journalists are more interested in sensationalism and making a big name for themselves in the media than in honestly reporting news events. Ever since the Watergate "media event," many journalists seem to have discarded journalistic ethics in favor of yellow journalism and muckraking.

The *Washington Post* Gets Nailed for Libel

Mobil Oil president William Tavoulareas scored a victory against press bias in July of 1982 when he was awarded $2.5 million in damages for a story published in the *Post* in 1979 (the *Post* appealed the decision).

In a speech to a national society of journalists meeting in Milwaukee in November, 1982, Tavoulareas asserted that if journalists "continue to refuse to condemn the practices which have caused the reduction of the media's credibility with the public, and if they refuse to consider a process for developing voluntary standards for behavior, then the day will come when the press will no longer be free."[3]

Unfortunately, the *Post* won its appeal. On May 2, 1983, a federal judge in Washington, D.C., overturned the award won by Tavoulareas.

The Canadian Press May Get a Watchdog

Journalists have always prided themselves on being the so-called watchdogs of government. Supposedly representing freedom, they act to insure that government does not infringe on our Constitutional rights. But no group or organization is available to watch over these "watchdogs." To remedy abuses of the press in Canada, the federal government has recently proposed the establishment of a National Press Council. As planned, this council would have no regulatory powers; it would rely on the power of public opinion to influence the press.

As a result of this proposal, journalists throughout Canada now form their own voluntary councils to deal with complaints against the media. While the Canadian government is probably taking a positive step by establishing this National Press Council, I am somewhat skeptical about the effect of the voluntary councils when staffed by journalists. That's like hiring a sex offender to run a nursery school.

The American Press Needs a Watchdog, Too!

I have felt for many years that America needs a media review board, much like the one being considered in Canada.

I realize that many newspapers maintain what they call an "ombudsman," who investigates complaints made against the newspaper by the public and acts as an impartial judge. Frankly, I consider the ombudsman concept a total fraud. How can a man who is probably drawing a $30,000 a year salary from the newspaper *really* investigate journalistic fraud in his own paper? I don't think that is possible.

Journalists are supposed to abide by a "code of ethics," but very few papers even have a written code to guide their employees. In a survey conducted by the Professional Standards Committee of the Associated Press Managing Editors in 1981, only thirty out of eighty-eight papers surveyed reported a written code of ethics.[4]

Some editors find a code of ethics for reporters distasteful. In a *Los Angeles Times* article, William F. Thomas, editor and executive vice-president of the *Times,* declared that the codes are "a bunch of platitudes. . . . I don't like to be treated like a child . . . and that's what those codes of ethics seem to say to me. . . . It's insulting."[5] By contrast, the public is incensed that the character of honorable people can be needlessly maligned and distorted because the press is not accountable to anyone but itself. The press policy at present is equivalent to having no policy at all.

Former CBS executive Fred W. Friendly has warned that journalists who stubbornly resist any self-regulation are behaving like many businessmen before the federal government passed the Sherman Antitrust Act. By arrogantly refusing to clean up their own act, they are inviting government intervention. According to Friendly, "When newspapers get on their high horses and say, 'We're different from everybody else; we are accountable only to ourselves, and that's somehow what the Constitution of the United States says,' that's almost a blasphemy."[6]

All papers should have a code of ethics. But such a code will do little if personal commitment to the code is lacking. As former *New York News* editor Michael O'Neill reminds us, "The fact is that no grievance committees or councils or laws will really work if the general attitude of the profession is not supportive. If the attitude is right, however, all the clanking machinery is probably unnecessary. Our best defense against opponents, our best bet for strengthening reader credibility, is an openness of mind that encourages both self-examination and outside criticism."[7] Even Warren Beatty thinks the press needs a watchdog. When speaking to the American Society of Newspaper Editors, he warned, "I don't think the press is tough enough on the press." He then suggested that newspapers create well-publicized boards that give a kind of reverse Pulitzer Prize for bad reporting. "Irresponsible journalism should . . . be pointed out by responsible journalists. If the press were a little tougher with each other, maybe the public or the judicial system would be a little less tough on the press."[8] However, we would expect a liberal-dominated review board to be so biased that it would see nothing wrong with distortions, so long as they advanced the liberal cause. They would approve liberal reporting, using media power to destroy the reputation of conservative ministers or politicians with whom they disagreed. Fairness and objectivity to a liberal means the freedom to attack what he considers the errors of conservatism or fundamentalism and, in many cases, the freedom to attack personalities without fear of libel suits. At the same time, anyone who points out his liberal bias must be branded a censor.

Asking the media to police itself is about as practical as asking Jesse James to verify gold at Fort Knox.

Let's Establish a Media Review Board

We simply cannot wait around for the attitude of America's liberal journalists to become more open to criticism. We need to institute media review boards operating at the local, state, and national level. A review board would not possess any authority to impose sanctions against the media, nor would it have the force of law. It would be designed primarily to serve as a pressure group, using the power of public opinion to bring about changes in the media.

I propose that this review board grade newspapers according to their ideological commitment, their fairness and objectivity. Our movies are graded G, PG, R, and X. Why not ask a review board to issue a report grading newspapers, radio, TV stations, and magazines based upon ideology, fairness, and objectivity?

The media review board I am advocating could be comprised of from five to seven members. It should be representative of the community where it is located and staffed by people who are respected and known for their impartiality in the community. On the national level, the president should appoint some members, with Congress appointing others. It might even be profitable for the vice-president to preside over this board; on the local level the mayor and city council could perform this task.

As I introduce the concept of a media review board, let me make one thing clear: I am just as concerned that liberals get a fair hearing in conservative publications as vice versa. The main difficulty, however, is that liberals have always enjoyed an overwhelming monopoly in the communications outlets in America and thus have virtually blacked out the conservative viewpoint.

The media review board should issue a "seal of approval," much like the *Good Housekeeping* seal, to media outlets that display a commitment to truth and fairness. It should also give special recognition to those newspapers, radio, TV stations, and magazines that have demonstrated excellence and honesty in reporting. This board should provide a "truth in communication" analysis that lists newspapers, and so on, according to their ideology. In that way, readers can make an honest evaluation of what they read in these publications.

The media review board, I repeat, would have no legislative powers, but should rely on massive publicity and public opinion to force a drastic change in the arrogant attitudes of the liberals who control the media in America.

Media liberals were the first to call for police review boards. They would love to censor our nation's law-enforcement officials and subject them to citizen surveillance. In fairness, these same liberal media professionals ought to call for a media review board—but I wouldn't count on it. Our hidden censors want the power to say what they wish with impunity.

The Awesome Power of the TV Monopolists

In November of 1969, then Vice-president Spiro Agnew fell into disfavor with the media elite by publicly attacking television and liberal press bias. At one point in his speech, he made the following remarks:

> Is it not fair and relevant to question its [media] concentration in the hands of a tiny enclosed fraternity of privileged men, elected by no one and enjoying a monopoly sanctioned and licensed by government? The views of the majority of this fraternity do not and I repeat—not—represent the views of America.
>
> As with other American institutions, perhaps it is time the networks were made more responsive to the views of the nation and more responsible to the people they serve. Now I want to make myself perfectly clear, I am not asking for government censorship or any other kind of censorship. I'm asking whether a form of censorship already exists when the news that 40 million Americans receive each night is determined by a handful of men responsible only to their corporate employers and is filtered through a handful of commentators who admit to their own set of biases.[1]

After studying the subject of media bias for many years and experiencing this bias firsthand, I couldn't agree with Agnew more. The basic premise of this chapter is simple: Early in this century, liberal/humanists gained significant control over radio and television. As a result of their seizure of our communications system, they have effectively censored out any conservative or Christian viewpoints.

The liberal/humanists who control our major communications systems continually cry "censorship" when any group attempts to modify the degrading programming they offer. In effect, they are refusing to be dethroned from their elitist position as *censor; they* want to maintain a blackout of any Christian or conservative viewpoint on television/radio or in the press.

A brief look at the history of NBC, CBS, and ABC will clarify how we arrived at our position today. We also must consider the entire philosophy motivating the "networks" to see if their goals are truly in the interest of the American viewer.

The Liberal/Humanists Seize Radio

Guglielmo Marconi is credited with having invented "wireless" technology. In 1894 Marconi transmitted radio signals for the first known time. In 1896 he headed for England to take out a patent on his revolutionary invention, and the year following he formed British Marconi to market his new product. It was his desire to create a world monopoly on his new invention: radio.[2]

By 1899 he had successfully transmitted messages across the English Channel; in 1901 he sent a signal across the Atlantic Ocean. As the wireless was perfected, it became obvious to Marconi and others that one of its most valuable uses would be communication between ships at sea.[3]

America was a logical market for radio, so in 1899 he instituted American Marconi. His driving goal was still to establish a worldwide monopoly, but he soon found himself under pressure by American interests to sell American Marconi to a group of businessmen.

According to one source: "British Marconi found itself subjected to an international squeeze play. The American government made no overt move actually to expropriate British Marconi's American holdings; the international negotiations were carried out on a private level by Owen D. Young of General Electric."[4]

We can only speculate as to what immense pressures were put on Marconi to surrender his assets in America. The president of American Marconi told his stockholders in 1919, "We have found that there exists on the part of the officials of the Government a very strong and irremovable objection to [American Marconi] because of the stock interest held therein by the British Company."[5]

In 1919 American Marconi sold its assets to the Radio Corporation of America, a newly formed organization established by Owen D. Young. As partners with Young of General Electric were American Telephone and Telegraph; Western Electric; Westinghouse; and the Tropical Radio Company, a subsidiary of the United Fruit Company.[6] RCA was soon to emerge as the strongest radio business in America.

Owen D. Young and the Council on Foreign Relations

Young was a vice-president of General Electric when he negotiated the takeover of American Marconi by RCA. He was also involved in international politics.

In 1924, for example, he was chosen to serve with Charles G. Dawes on a committee of experts dealing with German war reparations. By 1929 the Young Plan was approved by the allied nations, and the Bank for International Settlements was established.[7] During this period of history, Owen D. Young was intimately associated with the Council on Foreign Relations. In fact, according to historian Carroll Quigley, Young was an agent of the J. P. Morgan banking empire, and the CFR was simply a front group for the Morgan financial interests in America.

In Europe, the Morgan front was the Royal Institute for International Affairs. According to Quigley, "The New York branch was dominated by the associates of the Morgan Bank. For example, in 1928, the Council on Foreign Relations had John W. Davis as president, Paul Cravath as vice president, and a council of thirteen others, which included Owen D. Young. . . ."[8]

RCA and the Network System

David Sarnoff and RCA.   As a youth, David Sarnoff had been fascinated by the new "wireless" technology. As early as 1908, Sarnoff was working as a wireless operator on Nantucket Island, Massachusetts. Later he was hired by American Marconi in New York City. Starting his career as an office boy, he soon became a skilled wireless operator. As a point of historical interest, it was Sarnoff who had been on duty the night of the *Titanic* sinking, maintaining contact with the survivors of that tragedy. By 1916 he was a traffic manager with American Marconi.[9]

When RCA took over American Marconi in 1919, Sarnoff stayed on and apparently gained the confidence of Owen Young and the other co-owners of RCA. By 1930, David Sarnoff had become president of RCA; by 1947 he was chairman of the board. Sarnoff apparently had some help along the way.

According to Gary Allen and Larry Abraham, ". . . Most people do not know that the so-called founders of such giants as the *New York Times* and NBC were chosen, financed and directed by Morgan, Schiff and their allies. The case of Adolph Ochs of the *Times* and David Sarnoff of RCA are examples of this control. Both were given early financial aid by Kuhn, Loeb & Company and Morgan Guaranty."[10]

Kuhn, Loeb & Company was an American branch of the Rothschild international banking empire. Its head at the time was Jacob Schiff, who is credited with having given over $20 million to help Lenin and Trotsky consolidate their power in Russia.[11] It is my guess that Kuhn, Loeb & Company and the Morgan interests were confident that David Sarnoff would cooperate with them in maintaining a tight monopoly on the emerging technology of radio. Sarnoff, of course, was a long-time member of the Council on Foreign Relations.

NBC Is Organized as the First Network. In 1926 RCA founded the National Broadcasting Company. In the beginning it was a jointly owned venture, with RCA controlling 50 percent; General Electric, 20 percent; and Westinghouse, 20 percent.[12] By 1930, however, after both Westinghouse and GE had withdrawn, NBC became a wholly owned subsidiary of RCA, with Sarnoff as president.

It was the first company ever organized to be a broadcasting network. Because RCA had originally been co-owned by GE, American Telephone & Telegraph, and others, there were many diverse viewpoints about the operation of this fledgling broadcasting system. As a matter of fact, two groups emerged —the "radio" group and the "telephone" group—both with distinct philosophies about broadcasting.

The telephone group perceived radio broadcasting as a new kind of phone service. This group didn't feel that the network should have any responsibility or authority in determining what messages were sent over radio. They believed that radio should be a "common carrier," simply providing the technology for communication among individuals.[13]

The radio group, on the other hand, viewed broadcasting as a way of stimulating the marketplace for the sale of manufactured products. This group believed it should be responsible for supplying and controlling all messages going over radio.

If the telephone-group "common carrier" philosophy had prevailed during the early years of radio, we would probably not have a liberal/humanist media elite exercising so much power over what we see or hear. The system would have operated much the way the phone company does today. Any organization or group with enough money could purchase time on the network to express its viewpoint. But the radio-group philosophy eventually won out, and NBC quickly evolved into a money machine.

In the early years of radio, NBC operated only one network, but soon it added a second. These two networks were identified as the blue and red networks, after the colors used by engineers to trace the separate network coverages on national maps.[14]

Networks and the Airwaves

Networks and Independent Stations. Before we go any further, I should explain the difference between a *network* and an *independent station.* A network, whether established by ABC, CBS, NBC, or the Mutual Broadcasting System, is a group of stations which have agreed to affiliate with the parent broadcast organization. In exchange for this affiliation, the radio or TV station receives a certain amount of programming from the network each week.

At present, the three major TV networks have at least 200 affiliates receiving the same network programming. In fact, nearly 65 percent of all the programming on these once-independent stations is provided by the network. Big money is to be made by becoming a network affiliate. But once hooked, a local station has difficulty cutting itself free from the affiliation, primarily because too much money is involved. There are very few independent stations today in America; most have chosen to be spoon-fed by the major networks in exchange for millions of dollars in revenue generated through advertising.

In the early years of network radio, advertisers (or their agents) produced their own programs. But all of that changed in later years as the networks gained more and more control over the advertisers and program content.

A key point to remember about these networks is this: NBC, ABC, and CBS are *not* licensed by the Federal Communications Commission to broadcast *anything* over *our* airwaves. They are merely broadcasting services provided to local network affiliates. These local stations are licensed by the FCC to broadcast, and they are responsible for everything that goes out over their stations.

The FCC and the Radio Act of 1927. The Federal Communications Commission was established in 1934. Its job was to set guidelines and standards for the new broadcasting medium of radio and any future technologies. Born out of the Radio Act of 1927, the FCC was directed to regulate the new technology in accordance with a specific set of principles. These principles were as follows: Radio waves or channels belong to the people; broadcasting is a unique service; service must be equitably distributed; not everyone is eligible even to use a channel. Radio broadcasting is a form of expression protected by the First Amendment; the government has discretionary regulatory powers, although they are not absolute.[15]

With these concepts in mind, the FCC began licensing radio stations and establishing carefully defined procedures for broadcasting.

The primary principle to keep in mind is that *the airwaves belong to the people*—not to the local stations and certainly not to the networks. The stations are licensed to use the airwaves only as long as they serve the public interest. When it become obvious to the local citizenry that a station is not serving the public interest, they can demand an investigation by the FCC, which, in turn, can refuse to renew the license of a local station. Unfortunately this seldom happens.

By providing over 60 percent of the programming for local stations, the major networks have successfully achieved monopolistic control of our communications system. This is in direct violation of the original intent of the Radio Act of 1927, which states that we, the people, own the airwaves. Yet the networks have controlled *our* airwaves to satisfy their own corporate greed and to censor out opposing political or religious viewpoints.

The Founding of the Columbia Broadcasting System

William S. Paley has been firmly in control of CBS since he purchased the ailing network back in 1928 with a fortune he had made in his family's business, the Congress Cigar Company. At the age of twenty-six, he invested nearly half a million dollars in CBS, then called the United Independent Broadcasters.[16]

An astute businessman and a longtime member of the Council on Foreign Relations, Paley quickly devised an ingenious way of attracting independent stations to his network. In his autobiography, *As It Happened,* Paley reported, "I proposed the concept of free sustaining service; that is, to make the sustaining programs available to the affiliates at no cost."[17] He guaranteed his affiliates twenty hours of programming each week and agreed to pay them fifty dollars an hour for the commercial hours used. The network would sell advertising within these programs and the local stations could sell advertising as well. In exchange for free programming, noted Paley, ". . . We were to have exclusive rights for network broadcasting through the affiliate. That meant the local station could not use its facilities for any other broadcasting network."[18]

These independent stations, licensed by the FCC to serve the public interest, willingly gave up their independence to the network monopolists. In providing this programming to the local stations, Paley had gained control of a large segment of our communications system—for his own political and personal aggrandizement.

For a time, Paramount Pictures was part owner of CBS, but eventually Paley bought back control of the corporation. In these negotiations, Paley hired the services of three international banking firms to handle the negotiations: Brown Brothers, Harriman; Lehman Brothers; and Field, Glore.[19]

In his autobiography, Paley states that as soon as the Paramount directors resigned, he immediately appointed four new directors, three of them from Wall Street banking firms. Apparently one of these new directors was Arthur H. Bunker of Lehman Brothers.[20] Bunker, a CFR member, was also an official in the United World Federalists, a group whose stated purpose is "To create a world federal government with authority to enact, interpret, and enforce world law adequate to maintain peace."[21]

Paley's broadcasting empire now includes not just CBS, but Holt, Rinehart and Winston, a leading publisher of elementary, high school, and college textbooks; W. B. Saunders Company, the world's leading publisher of medical textbooks; Popular Library, Inc.; Creative Playthings; Wonder Products; Bailey Films Inc. and Film Associates of California, producers of educational films and filmstrips for schools, colleges, and libraries; Steinway and Sons, the piano company; and much more.[22]

The Birth of ABC

While NBC and CBS were vying for advertising dollars and new affiliates, the Mutual Broadcasting Network was struggling to survive. In 1938, at the urging of Mutual, the FCC began an investigation of NBCs blue and red networks to determine if they were being operated in the public interest.[23]

The investigators concluded that NBC should sell one of its networks. In 1943 it sold its blue network to Edward J. Noble, the president of the Lifesaver candy company. Noble, a Unitarian, served initially in the FDR administration as head of the Civil Aeronautics Authority and later was chosen by Secretary of Commerce Harry Hopkins to be his top assistant as Undersecretary of Commerce.[24]

Two other interested parties had bid on the blue network, but Noble won. Paramount Pictures, represented by Dillon, Read Company (a CFR-related international banking firm) and Marshall Field tried to buy the network. Field was a radical leftist newspaper publisher who owned papers in Chicago and New York.[25]

After Noble purchased the blue network, he changed its name to the American Broadcasting Company. ABC floundered financially for years after, but finally, on the verge of collapse, it came under the control of United Paramount Pictures in 1953. The man who had orchestrated this merger was a lawyer for Paramount, Leonard H. Goldenson. With this new arrangement, Goldenson became the president of ABC-Paramount and Edward Noble was chairman of the Finance Committee.[26]

How the Networks Maintain Their Monopoly

In a *New York Times* article, Everett C. Parker, director of the Office of Communications of the United Church of Christ, focused in on the dangers of network monopoly control.

He observed:

> ... It was never the intention of the Congress to have programming become the monopoly of three gigantic national corporations that can force their product on local stations willy-nilly with economic annihilation as the alternative ... nor to have prime-time programs aimed only at the limited audience of people between 18 and 49, as the networks now do, excluding the rest. Today the average network-affiliated television station has no control over 65 percent of its programs. At best, it can only say yes or no to the networks; it has little influence on network decisions.[27]

Control of Network Affiliates

Whatever appears on your television screen can be effectively controlled by one of three men: the heads of ABC, CBS, and NBC. If they do not want you to see something, you will not see it. This control, of course, is not a result of our free-enterprise system in action. Indeed, as A. Frank Reel declared, " 'Free Enterprise' in this case is a euphemism for what is the most powerful, most effective, and most impregnable monopoly in the history of the United States: the television-network monopoly."[28]

As stated earlier, when a station signs on as an affiliate of a network, it gives up its responsibilities to operate in the public interest. Being an affiliate is worth literally millions to a station, and thus, station managers only reluctantly buck the system. Profit is the name of the game.

The programmers at the networks aim to please four groups, in this order: their stockholders, the advertisers, the FCC, and finally the public. As long as the affiliates and the network make money, it really doesn't matter if the public interest is not being served.

Controlling the Advertisers

In the early years of radio broadcasting and on into the era of television, sponsors or advertising agencies produced their own programs or controlled segments of time on the networks. It was common for a sponsor to put on high quality programs. Remember Kraft Music Hall, Armstrong Circle Theater, the Colgate Hour, and others?

The sponsors were not obsessed by ratings and demographics in those days. They were interested in providing something of quality, and they hoped to build up a loyal audience, even if that audience was small.

By 1959, however, the networks had decided that they would no longer permit sponsors to own or control advertising time on programs.[29] Today a sponsor can rarely put on his own program. There are occasional "specials," but these are the exceptions. Under the current rules of the media monopolists, the advertiser can only purchase thirty- to sixty-second spots with programs. Very often the advertiser will just tell his agent what audience he wants to reach and in what time periods. The agent will contact the network, and a network computer will pick the days and times for the advertising to appear.[30]

As TV executive Bob Shanks reports, "An advertiser's power to control or affect programming is reaction rather than action. When presented with a program idea or schedule not to his liking, the advertiser can refuse to buy in."[31] Although the sponsor does not directly control what is shown on television, he *can* bring about a change in the content of current programming by *refusing* to advertise on immoral shows.

Ratings. In the mind of the media monopolists, you and I are not human beings; we are a *product* that is sold to the advertiser, who purchases time on TV based on the ratings—or how many million homes are tuned into a particular show. The higher the ratings, the higher the advertising rates—more money for the TV monopolists.

Ratings determine if a show will remain on the air. No matter how well done or how important a show might be, if it doesn't grab at least a 30 percent rating, it will most likely be axed by the network. A 30 percent rating means that out of a total of 68.5 million homes with televisions, 30 percent of those were tuned in to the program.

Ratings are determined by the A. C. Nielsen Company, Arbitron, or Trendex. The most visible of these three is the Nielsen rating,[32] which consults the viewing habits of no more than 1,200 families in America. Each "Nielsen family" is equipped with a little black box, which is attached to the television. This box automatically records the viewing habits of that particular family. It may seem incredible, but a television show usually lives or dies by these 1,200 families.

Demographics. Network executives and advertisers are interested in the demographics of the population—that is, the sex, age, and buying habits of the TV viewers. In order to sell their products, the advertisers must aim at a certain segment of the market. Most TV programs are produced to attract women between the ages of eighteen and forty-nine, because they spend the most money in America. If you happen to be under eighteen or older than forty-nine, the monopolists don't really care if you exist. They are only concerned with profits.

In his autobiography, William Paley relates how his marketing officials had advised him to upgrade his programming in the early 1970s. "These officials warned him that his audience had 'skewed' old, meaning he had to revamp his schedule by appealing to a much younger audience." During this meeting, one of his more compassionate researchers started to cry. " 'You don't know what you're doing,' he exclaimed. 'You're throwing away millions and millions of viewers.' "[33]

It didn't matter. The schedule was revamped to attract a younger audience, callously discarding millions of older viewers.

"The Lawrence Welk Show" fell victim to this kind of thinking back in 1971. ABC canceled the show, even though it had a large audience, for the programmers reported that it "skewed old," meaning that it was enjoyed by men and women who had lived past forty-nine years of age.[34] Fortunately, Welk's producer, Don Federson, syndicated the program on 150 stations, and the show did very well on into the 1980s, when Welk retired.

People Don't Watch Programs—They Watch "Television"

Television has become a pervasive influence in our lives. It is treated like a member of the family in many households. Before the advent of radio or television, families would gather in the living room for the evening to talk or read. But today in many homes, the television has taken the place of any meaningful relationships among family members.

Television has been given a variety of nicknames, such as the boob tube, the idiot box, and the plug-in drug. It has been likened to "chewing gum for the eyes." A recent book on television, written by Tony Schwartz, a professor of telecommunications at New York University, is called *Media: The Second God.* Schwartz points out, "The media are all-knowing. They supply a community of knowledge and feelings, and a common morality.... Godlike, the media can change the course of a war, bring down a president or a king, elevate the lowly and humiliate the proud, by directing the attention of millions on the same event and in the same manner."[35]

Americans have been so conditioned by television that it no longer matters what program is on. People watch it, not because program content interests them, but simply because its presence pervades the living room. In many homes the television is on all day long, even if no one watches it.

Television acts as a very seductive force in our homes. Because people are almost mesmerized by the color and sound being projected from the set, advertisers and programmers continually exploit the public's psychological addiction to television. These men know, for example, that regardless of what is transmitted from any of the stations in the evening, at least 70 million Americans will automatically turn on their sets at 7:30 P.M. This number will rise steadily until it reaches 90 to 100 million by 9:00 P.M.[36] They can be certain that an audience will worship at the shrine of television every evening. What they don't know is what show will lure the largest number of viewers on any particular night.

Paul Klein, now an executive with the Playboy Channel, spent years at NBC, first as a vice-president in charge of audience measurement and later as a vice-president of programming. He has an interesting theory about viewer addiction, the "LOP" theory (the Least Objectionable Program).[37] He believes people will watch *anything,* but they are motivated to view what is most tolerable of all operative choices. They do not select the *best,* but what is least offensive or most relaxing. His theory probably has an element of truth in it. I know that in presidential elections, millions of people have voted for the "lesser of two evils" in the same manner. When given a selection of three totally irrelevant situation comedies, the viewer can choose to turn the set off or pick the one that is least obnoxious. That is hardly freedom of choice.

The Audience Flow

One firmly entrenched belief among television programmers is called audience flow, the commonly held notion that TV audiences are notoriously lazy. Once they begin to watch a station early in the evening, the station must feed them similar programming throughout the remainder of the night or lose them to another station. There is nothing worse for ratings than to put a scholarly documentary on pelicans between "Laverne and Shirley" and "Three's Company." The anesthetized viewer will switch the dial to the competitor's station in order to watch another inane sitcom.

All three networks operate on the audience-flow theory. As a result, the viewer, who supposedly owns the airwaves, is subjected to selections of mindless drivel or supermindless drivel. There are exceptions to this, of course, but television is not primarily concerned about quality. It focuses chiefly upon profits and ideology.

What Will the Future Bring?

Some drastic changes seem to be taking place in the television industry these days, due in large measure to the so-called video revolution. It appears that Americans are beginning to switch off the networks in favor of other forms of electronic entertainment.

In 1982, for example, an estimated 1.5 million viewers decided they would prefer other offerings than the pap churned out by the three networks. According to Bill Behanna, director of press relations for the A. C. Nielsen Co., "The assumption, until we know better, is that they're going to non-network sources. That would mean pay cable, basic cable, independent stations, public stations and cassette recorders."[38]

One of the greatest beneficiaries of this mass desertion of network programming is the Public Broadcasting System. In October of 1982, PBS officials announced that their viewing audience had increased by 50 percent in the previous year.[39] PBS has profited from being broadcast over many cable systems as well.

Cable and pay TV services are also gaining added viewers. Jay Campbell, president of Cable Ad Ventures, notes, "Clearly cable is drawing audiences. . . . With a box full of channels, the viewer is flipping around. Cable is offering unique programs that give viewers alternatives."[40]

Even though average television viewing time is increasing, the major networks receive a smaller portion of the audience. According to Tony Schwartz, "Compared with last year, the three networks have declined more than 2 rating points—each of which represents 800,000 homes and is worth close to $50 million a year. In terms of their share of the total viewing audience, the networks have declined from 86.7 percent to 83.1 percent."[41] The advertising firm of Ogilvy & Mather has predicted that today's networks will lose more viewers by 1990, when the number of Americans watching network TV will shrink to less that 40 percent of the viewing audience.[42]

Loss of viewers means loss of revenue and potential financial disaster for the networks. It also means that we might see an end to the TV monopolists' empire. NBC's Grant Tinker recently observed, "People may simply have lost patience with network fare. Maybe they're looking for something new on cable, or something old and good on the independents. Maybe they're reading books or going to sleep. . . ."[43]

I am optimistic about the advances taking place in cable television, but it is going to take more than a video revolution to break the monopolists' hold on our airwaves. Only concerted public pressure can *force* the networks to release their stranglehold on the network affiliates.

The Hollywood Cesspool

They say this is a dope town, but then, we live in a dope nation now. There's no discipline, no love of work, no standards, little kindness. I'm lucky I'm not starting out now. The whole movie industry is out in space somewhere. There's no romance, no love. And the sex scenes in today's pictures, I just don't believe it. We were never faced with that problem.[1]

In her interview in *Parade* magazine (March, 1983), Bette Davis expressed her disillusionment and shock at what has happened to the Hollywood she once knew and loved. She voiced sympathy for the young women who, in attempting to find appropriate roles as actresses, are being mercilessly exploited. As she observed, "I think that if most of the girls today turned down these sex scenes, they wouldn't get any jobs. And they're not even *love* scenes. They just *do* it, which I find totally unattractive. Romance is gone, and that's what the public misses the most."[2]

Bette Davis and other actresses of the "golden years" were spared the degradation of appearing nude, but Hollywood has always been a center of immorality in America. According to film historian Arthur Knight, by 1922 Hollywood had become known as the most glamorous and most corrupt city in the country. The young actors and actresses who had flocked to Hollywood had become too rich, too fast. Not mature enough to handle this sudden wealth, they squandered fortunes on booze, drugs, and high living.

The Hollywood film producers of the 1920s were quick to capitalize on what they saw as a "new morality" in American culture, so they filled the screens with sex, violence, alcohol and drug abuse. They soon discovered to their horror, however, that the "new morality" so common in the big cities had not yet infected the rest of the nation. Ministers of the Gospel, politicians, and grass-roots organizations loudly protested the flagrant immorality being shown in the movies.

To protect their profits and to avoid censorship by the federal government, the heads of the major movie studios quickly formed the Motion Picture Producers and Distributors of America in 1922. This organization had two formidable tasks ahead of it: to fight off efforts to impose national censorship on the movie industry and to set up some reasonable guidelines for self-censorship within the industry. To accomplish these tasks, they appointed as president Will H. Hays, a Presbyterian elder who was also a chairman of the Republican National Committee and was serving as postmaster general in the Harding administration when he was appointed.[3]

By 1927 Hays had developed a set of guidelines to be followed by the movie producers. However, as the public furor died down, the producers became bolder and bolder in what they showed on the screen.

In 1930, to combat this new upsurge of immorality, Martin Quigley, a Chicago publisher of film trade magazines, joined forces with Father Daniel Lord, S. J., to rewrite Hays's guidelines into a carefully constructed motion-picture production code.[4] To put additional pressure on the movie industry, Quigley organized the Legion of Decency in 1934. Through the considerable influence of the legion, the Motion Picture Producers and Distributors of America established a production code administration, under the direction of a Roman Catholic layman, Joseph I. Breen.[5]

Christian Principles Are Embodied in the Production Code

The production code developed by Quigley, Father Lord, and the Legion of Decency established three general principles: No picture was to be produced that would tend to lower the moral standards of those watching it; only correct standards of life, subject to the needs of drama and entertainment, were to be presented; the forces of law and order were never to be ridiculed, and evil was never to be made attractive.[6]

Here are some excerpts from this now-defunct Motion Picture Production Code: "No film or episode may throw ridicule on any religious faith. . . . Pictures shall not infer that low forms of sex relationships are the accepted or common thing . . . the sympathy of the audience shall never be thrown to the side of crime, wrongdoing, evil or sin. . . . Brutal killings are not to be presented in detail. . . . Complete nudity is never permitted."[7]

Amazingly enough, this excellent production code was maintained by the film industry from 1934 through 1966, when it was gutted. Without public pressure placed on the industry, I believe there would have been no production code, and the movie industry would have given the public an endless string of movies depicting gross sexual sin, murders, rapes, and graphic sexual violence—exactly what the industry is spewing forth today in the absence of self-restraint.

The production code was effectively destroyed when Jack Valenti became president of the Motion Picture Association of America (the new name of the MPPDA). Valenti, a liberal, had been one of Lyndon Johnson's close personal advisors before joining the MPAA. He quickly discarded the old production code and issued a new "Code of Self-Regulation" on September 20, 1966.[8] In November of 1968 he established a movie rating system, using G, PG, R, and X to indicate the content of each movie.[9]

With this new "code" and the rating system in place, the movie industry tossed off self-censorship and has embarked on an orgy of "self-expression." The current themes in movies today include brutal gang warfare, occult horror, homosexuality, pro-Communist "message films," ultraviolence, rape, and nudity.

We only have to peruse the evening newspaper's "entertainment" section to realize just how debased the movies have become. The typical producer or director of these gross films will glibly explain that he is only concerned about "reality." Actually, many of these producers and directors are spiritually sick men, acting out their own perverted fantasies through their films.

Martin Scorsese, director of such vile films as *Taxi Driver, Mean*

Streets, and others, has admitted that his movies are therapy for his personal "anger and rage and craziness."[10] Scorsese concedes, "These are morality plays for myself. . . . I've just found myself lucky to be able to express my personal feelings on film, because that's my medium."[11] His films invariably deal with loneliness, guilt, alienation, violence, death, emptiness.

Scorsese, like so many of his fellow directors and producers in Hollywood, is a man without hope in this world. Yet he is a man of immense power, using the medium of film to communicate to the world his own sense of meaninglessness. Instead of finding a catharsis for his personal feelings of emptiness and guilt in a private journal or diary, he displays his personal anguish for the world to see—and *imitate.*

Without the production code providing a sound moral structure for the movie industry, Hollywood has been invaded by a new breed of filmmaker: hollow, godless men driven by lust for fame and fortune and obsessed with a need for "self-expression." But instead of imprinting their obscene thoughts on bathroom walls, they have chosen to produce blatantly obscene films.

Hollywood Reverts to the Dark Ages

Diane Jacobs, author of *Hollywood Renaissance,* applauds this new breed of filmmaker. She details their lives and films in her book, pleased that they have cast off the taboos of society. Men like Robert Altman, John Cassavetes, Francis Ford Coppola, Paul Mazursky, Martin Scorsese, and others have led the film industry into this so-called renaissance. Jacobs's tribute, we should note, is quite appropriate, because the Italian Renaissance was a rebirth of godless humanism in Europe and a rejection of traditional Christian morality.

The Hollywood Renaissance likewise represents a return to barbarism and spiritual darkness. Our humanistic filmmakers have allowed themselves the total freedom to degrade, ridicule, and destroy everything good in man. They have done their best to convince their audiences of man's irrelevance in nature. From their sickly existential viewpoint, man is nothing. He is destined to be born, to suffer, and to die.

One of the most frightening displays of humanistic obscenity is *Bad*

Boys, produced by Robert Solo and released in theaters early in 1983. The ultraviolence in this feature is mind numbing. Solo has chosen to graphically show a man beaten with a lead pipe, the savage rape of a high-school girl, and close-ups of a knife being repeatedly jabbed through a victim's leg. But Solo smugly asserts that "this is not a film about violence." He claims that this is a statement "about redemption and growth and hope. We've seen a lot of movies with gratuitous violence. Nothing in this film is gratuitous, from our point of view. It's there for a reason."[12]

Solo and his fellow filmmakers feel they can justify the most terrifying cruelties in their films—as long as they are not "gratuitous." In other words, if the violence somehow fits in with the plot, nothing is too gory, too bloody, too vile to show.

These producers all claim to be committed to "truth" and "reality" in their films, but that's a lie. Only *their* particular view of the world—a universe of chaos, violence, and death—surges from the screen. It is a cruel world of their own making, a hideous foretaste of hell.

Frank Capra Attacks the Hollywood Renaissance

Frank Capra, probably one of the finest filmmakers this country has ever known, gave us such wonderful movies as *It Happened One Night, It's a Wonderful Life, Mr. Smith Goes to Washington, Pocketful of Miracles,* and many more.

Capra believed in spiritual truth, in the innate dignity of man, and one's infinite value in the sight of God. As Capra remarked in his autobiography:

> Someone should keep reminding Mr. Average Man that he was born free, divine, strong; uncrushable by fate, society, or hell itself; and that he is a child of God, equal heir of all the bounties of God; and that goodness is riches, kindness is power, and freedom is glory. Above all, every man is born with an inner capacity to take him as far as his imagination can dream or envision—providing he is *free* to dream and envision.[13]

Capra, of course, has become concerned about the decline of morality in Hollywood's films. He observes, ". . . The giants are mostly gone.

The Marquis de Sade took over in the Sixties. . . . Almost everything else has been creep-hero stuff; glorifications of the 'minus' people or apologies for the 'brute' people. Gone the power of morality, of courage, of beauty, of the great love story."[14]

In the place of heroes arise antiheroes; in place of love we are inundated with lust and fornication. Morality has been subverted by situational ethics, sincerity by scoffing and cynicism.

Empty men like Martin Scorsese and Solo are leaders in the Hollywood Renaissance. Their films glorify the "minus" people and the brutes of our culture. But what motivates these producers and directors to make films about emptiness, alienation, and violence? What are their moral and political beliefs? We will discover what these men think about the world around them in the section on the Hollywood elite, but first we need to review the early financial and political history of the movie industry.

The Monopolists Seize Power

By the 1920s the movie industry was considered to be big business—so big, in fact, that J. P. Morgan; Kuhn, Loeb & Company; and other international banking firms had moved into the business to gain control over it.

One of the first true "movie Moguls" was Adolph Zukor, a New York theater owner who had formed the Famous Players group in 1913. According to Robert Sklar, Zukor's best ally in building his theater empire was a man named Otto Kahn, an astute investment banker with Kuhn, Loeb. (Kahn, like his friend Owen D. Young, was also an official in the Council on Foreign Relations by 1928.)[15]

With Otto Kahn's help, Kuhn, Loeb sold $10 million worth of preferred stock in Zukor's company, putting Zukor on a sound financial footing. From 1919 to 1921, Zukor acquired control of over 600 theaters.[16]

The international banking firms gained subtle domination of the movie industry either through financing or through the control of important equipment patents. According to Eric Rhode, many studios were forced to obtain equipment from two companies interested in gaining control of the movie industry: Western Electric, a subsidiary of

AT&T "almost entirely controlled by the J. P. Morgan group and holding assets of $30 billion" or "RCA Photophone, a subsidiary of RCA of America largely controlled by the Rockefeller empire through the Chase National Bank."[17]

During the financial disaster of the 1930s, Wall Street banking firms called in many of their loans to the major studios and simply took over those who could not repay. In *Money Behind the Screen,* published in 1937, authors F. D. Klingender and Stuart Legg observed that the motion-picture industry had been seized by "the most powerful financial groups in the United States, if not the capitalist world, the Morgans and the Rockefellers."[18] They also noted, "All the pioneer executives, except William Fox and Carl Laemmle, had allowed the financial control of their enterprises to slip out of their hands into those of their backers."[19]

Today many of the major studios are under the control of multinational corporations. Paramount is owned by Gulf & Western; Warner Brothers, by Kinney; United Artists, by TransAmerica; MGM, by a hotel magnate[20]; and Columbia Pictures by the Coca-Cola Company.

Communists Invade Hollywood

Lenin knew the immense propaganda value of film. Within two years after the overthrow of the Czarist government, Lenin took firm control of the film industry. He appointed Anatoli Lunacharsky, a playwright and film director, to head up the State Schools of Cinematography in Petrograd. Lenin told Lunacharsky that "of all the arts, for us the cinema is the most important."[21]

Lenin also knew that if he wanted to influence public opinion in America, he needed Communist agents inside the movie industry. He apparently had no trouble finding subversives willing to spread Communist propaganda through films.

William Ward Kimple served as an undercover agent working for the Los Angeles Police Department's Intelligence Squad, keeping tabs on Communist agents in the movie industry. He worked within the party from 1928 through 1939, eventually becoming a membership chairman. In 1955 he told the House Committee on Un-American Activities that he was "in the position . . . to positively identify the Communist Party membership of close to a thousand people" within the film industry.[22]

It has been estimated that between 1936 and 1947, at least 145 top Hollywood screenwriters were working for the Communist cause.[23] And many of these subversives were interrogated during House Committee on Un-American Activities hearings during the late 1940s and early 1950s.

The Hollywood Ten. The most famous of these subversives came to be known as the "Hollywood Ten." Today, if you try to find any accurate information about these men in books or magazines, you will invariably be fed the standard liberal line that they were noble, courageous men, taking a stand against McCarthyism in America. From our controlled press, you will *never* learn that these men were traitors to their country, that as Communists, they were sworn to the violent overthrow of our nation, and that they used their prestigious positions as screenwriters to push Communist propaganda.

The Hollywood Ten included John Howard Lawson, Alvah Bessie, Dalton Trumbo, Lester Cole, Albert Maltz, Samuel Ornitz, Ring Lardner, Jr., Herbert Biberman, Adrian Scott, and Edward Dmytryk.[24] All were sentenced to jail. Eight spent a year in a minimum security prison for contempt of Congress; two served six-month terms. All were fined a mere $1,000.[25]

Since their exposure as Communist subversives, these men have maintained to this day that their careers were ruined because of a so-called blacklist. But the truth is that nearly all of them have had continued access to Hollywood, writing many screenplays under pseudonyms. In 1952, for example, director Edward Dmytryk signed a lucrative four-year contract with Stanley Kramer at Columbia Pictures. Dmytryk directed such Kramer films, as *The Sniper, Eight Iron Men, The Juggler,* and *The Caine Mutiny.*[26]

Lester Cole, another member of the Hollywood Ten, has continued to enjoy a successful career as a screenwriter. Yet at seventy-seven he still maintains that a blacklist destroyed his career. Leonard Chassman, executive director of the Screenwriters Guild, disagrees. "The fact of the matter is that some writers who were well-known to have been blacklisted in the late 40's and early '50s have recovered their careers and are working in the business successfully today . . ."[27]

Cole, who willingly admits joining the party in 1934, has spent the last thirty years writing films, teaching film criticism at the University of California, Berkeley campus. Cole, for example, wrote the screenplays for *Born Free* and *Every Man for Himself.* One can only wonder how many more movies and television series have been produced in recent years by this dedicated Communist revolutionary.

Or take the example of Carl Foreman. Although not one of the Hollywood Ten, screenwriter Foreman was a hostile witness during HCUA hearings and repeatedly took refuge behind the Fifth Amendment when asked about his Communist Party affiliations. Six witnesses, in sworn testimony, identified Foreman as a dedicated party member.[28] Foreman has written several Stanley Kramer films, among them *High Noon, Home of the Brave, Cyrano de Bergerac,* and *So This Is New York.*[29]

Ring Lardner, Jr., did not suffer from any blacklist either. He went on to write *The Adventures of Robin Hood* for TV. Perhaps his most infamous accomplishment is the screenplay for the antiwar movie *M*A*S*H*,* directed by Robert Altman.

The Media Takes Care of Its Own

Proven radical leftists are not permitted to fail. Unlike fundamental Christians, who tend to shoot their own wounded, the left comes to the aid of its fallen heroes.

A classic example of the loyalty of the left was revealed immediately after the 1982 elections. Actors Charlton Heston and Paul Newman squared off on national television over the nuclear freeze issue during the last days of the campaign. Heston, who favored "peace, through strength," made liberal Newman look quite foolish for wanting to trust the Russians to keep a nuclear freeze treaty, even if they signed one. When Heston confronted handsome Paul with the fact that the Russians have broken at least fifty-two signed treaties, the latter indicated that he was unaware of such a statistic and, furthermore, refused to believe it. So Heston pulled the list out of his pocket and presented it to him. No wonder, according to a radio report, Heston said before the debate that Newman started talking in defense of the nuke freeze before he had his brain engaged.

Two weeks later *Time* magazine came to the rescue of its champion's tarnished image by putting his picture on the front cover with the caption, "Quite a Guy." What do *Time* and Newman have in common? On a scale of zero to ten, both would rate one. If you watch liberals to conservatives carefully, you will find many illustrations of how the left takes care of its own.

The Cesspool and Drug Use

Marijuana is passe nowadays in Hollywood. The drug of choice today is cocaine. Drug dealers commonly ride to the studios in limousines and peddle their drugs routinely on many movie and television sets. From the executives down to the technicians, "Coke is it!"

In fact, the abuse of this drug is so widespread now in the movie industry that many movie insurance companies are rewriting their policies to protect themselves against drug-related accidents. Under investigation at this writing is the tragic death of Vic Morrow and two Vietnamese children, who were killed when a helicopter crashed on them during the filming of an episode for *Twilight Zone*. Vic Morrow's children have filed a suit charging that illicit drug use on the set caused their father's death.[30]

Many non-drug users in Hollywood contend that the quality of the productions is being severely hampered by rampant drug use. One studio production vice-president alleged, "When the director or stars or producer are on cocaine, they seem to have tunnel vision. There's a party going on on-screen, but the audience isn't invited. You can't enter into the logic of the film. The sin is the mess that results on the screen."[31]

In recent years several actors, actresses, and directors have been arrested for drug use. John Belushi died of a drug overdose in March of 1982, and Richard Pryor nearly burned to death when his face caught fire as he prepared a potent drug mixture several years ago. Richard Dreyfuss almost died in a car accident while under the influence of cocaine.

According to Lieutenant Ed Hawkins of the Los Angeles Police Department, cocaine use in Hollywood is "at epidemic stages."[32]

Who Are the Hollywood Elite?

Drug abuse is merely a symptom of the deep spiritual vacuum that exists in the hearts of the Hollywood elite. Just what do these people want out of life? Where do they stand on moral and political issues?

Ben Stein, a former television screenwriter, has answered many of these questions for us in his book, *The View From Sunset Boulevard,* published in 1979. Stein was a *Wall Street Journal* film and TV critic who moved to California not long after graduating from Yale Law School. At one point in his writing career, he taught a course on the political and social content of film at the University of California at Santa Cruz.

Out of sheer boredom, he began watching television and soon discovered something that fascinated him. He noticed that the same political and social messages were being presented over and over again in nearly every show he viewed. To satisfy his curiosity, he interviewed forty influential writers and producers, eager to determine whether their own personal views were directly reflected in the content of the TV programs they worked on.

In his lengthy interviews he asked these writers and producers to describe how they felt about the military, the clergy, poor people, policemen, government officials, small towns, big cities, crime, businessmen, and the superrich.

Stein observed, ". . . The fit between the message of the TV shows and the opinions of the people who make the TV shows was excellent."[33] He added, "The super-medium of television is spewing out the messages of a few writers and producers (literally in the low hundreds), almost all of whom live in Los Angeles. Television is not necessarily a mirror of anything besides what these few people think."[34]

His book confirms what many of us have suspected for years: Movies and television do not mirror our culture. Rather, they are being used as propaganda tools to brainwash us into accepting the moral, political, and social views of only a few hundred embittered writers and producers.

According to Stein, there are no more than 200 writers and producers who create nearly everything you and I see in the movies or on television. And at the time of his writing, only about a dozen contractors produced programming for the major networks: Universal, MTM, Tandem/TAT, MGM, 20th Century Fox, Paramount, Quinn/Martin Productions, and Spelling/Goldberg.[35]

What were the general characteristics of these powerful TV writers and producers? Stein found nearly all of them to be white males. They were generally over thirty-five, never second-generation Californians; a large number of them came from New York and thought of themselves as politically "progressive."[36]

Usually they were violently opposed to businessmen, especially those in big business. Jim Brooks, producer of the "Mary Tyler Moore Show," "Lou Grant," and "Taxi," exclaimed that businessmen are "all cannibals ... They distrust people who are brilliant."[37]

Meta Rosenberg, producer of "The Rockford Files," viewed businessmen as part of a "dangerous concentration of power in America."[38]

Gary Marshal, producer of "Happy Days" and "Laverne and Shirley," said, "When the government says something, I'm never sure whether the government is telling the truth, or whether it's big business talking."[39]

A good number of TV moguls Stein questioned were convinced that the Mafia was in partnership with big business. One TV producer told Stein, "If you don't believe that the Mafia is running big business, you must be blind."[40]

Crime and Poor People

Stein, curious to learn their views on crime, found that they were not concerned about street crime, but sought to dramatize white-collar crime on televison. "In real life murders, rapes, and so forth, both victims and perpetrators are usually poor, minority-group people, apparently acting on sudden impulses of rage and anger."[41] But on television we seldom see the poor committing crime—or if we do, they are usually shown to be the fall guys for some rich businessman or gangland leader who simply exploits them for his own sinister purpose.

The Hollywood writers and producers Stein interviewed invariably agreed that poverty caused street crime. They consistently refused to hold the criminal responsible for his actions. As Stanley Kramer observed, "Crime comes from wars and repressions and ghettoes."[42] Bob Weiskopf remarked, "I suspect the bulk of the crimes are committed by people who are poor and oppressed."[43] His solution? Redistribution of the wealth.

Stein also discovered that in the minds of these writers and producers, poor people could do no wrong. In TV sitcoms, poor people nearly always appear as heroes or as victims of some cruel capitalist oppressor. They are never on welfare; they always tell the truth. They are well groomed and have wonderful senses of humor.

Is it any wonder that we find such a warped view of reality in movies and on television?

The Hollywood Elitists Rate Police and Military

Stein found confused opinions on policemen—contradictory feelings of love and hate, admiration and scorn. That confusion often is evident in police dramas. The main characters are usually sensitive, humorous, wise, and self-sacrificing. But those in positions above them are regularly either bungling idiots or willfully dishonest.

What about the elitists' views about the military? The range of opinions varied from seeing our defense system as a necessary evil to looking at the military with fear and disgust.

A high official at Norman Lear's production company told Stein, ". . . The people here are antiestablishment, and they see businessmen as part of the establishment, and they see the military as part of the establishment."[44]

Stein makes an interesting observation in his chapter on the military establishment. He recounts the storyline from a show called "Kingston: Confidential," starring Raymond Burr. In this particular episode, Burr discovers that a paramilitary group known as the American Action Clan has been working with an evil army general to divert weapons to be used in a right-wing uprising. The American Action Clan, as it turns out, is an offshoot of a militant fundamentalist religious sect.

The point of the show was obvious, Stein observed. The writers were making a clear connection between the military, the KKK, and Protestant fundamentalism. Unfortunately that view is seriously held by a good number of writers in Hollywood.

Government Bureaucrats Are Okay

Although the Hollywood elitists fear and hate the military, the FBI, and the CIA, they are generally fond of federal bureaucrats, who were viewed as decent people, if somewhat ineffectual in their tasks.

Stein observed, "One might suspect a general prostatism bias on the part of the writers and producers, but that would be hard to substantiate. While many spoke of redistribution of wealth in other contexts, no one said that the bureaucracy was well positioned to bring that about." Stein did note, however, that many of those he interviewed boasted of their leftist activities in their youth.[45]

The Elitists Hate Christianity

One of Stein's most fascinating chapters deals with the Hollywood elitists' view on religion and the clergy.

By and large, these writers and producers considered religion to be an irrelevant issue in America, playing no role in their lives. For instance, Stein interviewed Lee Rich, a producer who has given us "Dallas," "Flamingo Road," and others. When asked if the church was important in American life, Rich answered bluntly, "I gave up going to church at 17. I don't know anyone who goes to church." Rich is over sixty.[46]

Because the Hollywood writers and producers consider religion irrelevant, they simply censor religious characters out of TV altogether—unless of course, they need a Christian character to attack as a liar, hypocrite, whoremonger, embezzler, or buffoon.

Stein noted that those in Hollywood will usually leave Christians alone, except when they feel their power structure threatened by activist religious movements like the Moral Majority, Concerned Women for America, Christian Voice, or Donald Wildmon's Coalition for Better Television. It is permissible for Christians to play church, but as soon as we begin to take aggressive stands against homosexuality, abortion, and other immorality, the Hollywood crowd will go on the offensive, attacking Christianity through movies and television.

Franky Schaeffer makes this point:

> Granted, if the Christian is willing to stay in his little corner and do "religious activities" separated from the arts, industry, politics, science, law, economics, the media, or scholarship—in other words, all that really counts—then he is left to himself. As long as the Christian only sets out to convert souls, fine. But let him stand up and begin to challenge the dominant, humanistic forces and the press will make every attempt to either ignore or ravage that individual.[47]

Christians are threatening the power structure in Hollywood, so the media propagandists are fighting back through their television sitcoms, adventures and made-for-TV movies.

Ben Stein believes that Hollywood's writers, directors, and producers are also waging a war against the power centers in our nation—namely big business and the military. They seek to control our nation—even our minds. Stein warns, "By their intelligence and the power of technology, they stand astride the most powerful media instruments of all time. This tiny community in Hollywood has been given the fulcrum that can move the world—and its members know how to use it."[48]

Hollywood and America: The Odd Couple

Fortunately we now have solid statistical proof to verify Ben Stein's 1979 report. That evidence comes from a study conducted by researchers Linda S. Lichter, S. Robert Lichter, and Stanley Rothman, published in the December/January, 1983 issue of *Public Opinion* magazine.

In their research, they interviewed 104 of the most influential writers, producers, and executives in Hollywood. This sample included fifteen presidents of independent production companies, ten network vice-presidents of program development, forty-three producers, assorted writers, and story supervisors. In effect, they interviewed the cream of the crop in Hollywood.

What did these reseachers learn about the Hollywood elite? They found that 99 percent of them are white; 98 percent are males; 82 percent grew up in large metropolitan centers.[49] "...They are well educated, extraordinarily well paid, have adopted secular outlooks, and are politically very liberal."[50] One in four reported an income of over half a million dollars in 1981; 63 percent earned over $200,000. A mere 4 percent earned less than $75,000.

The majority of the Hollywood elite are humanists, although 93 percent of them had a religious upbringing. At present, however, 45 percent of them have no religious affiliation; 93 percent of them seldom or never attend religious services.[51]

Politically, they tend to be Democrats and liberal. According to 75 percent, they are left of center; only 14 percent claim to be right of center. The research team reminds us, "This contrasts sharply with the national picture. In a 1982 national poll, only 27 percent of the general public classified themselves as liberal, 32 percent termed themselves conservatives, and the remainder called themselves moderates."[52]

Their voting patterns reflect an extremely liberal view. In 1972, for example, the Hollywood elite favored McGovern by 82 percent, yet the *public* gave Richard Nixon 62 percent of the vote.[53] During the Reagan/Carter/Anderson presidential race, 49 percent voted for Carter, 27 percent for Anderson, and only 20 percent for Reagan.

Amorality Is the Name of the Game

The Hollywood elite and their counterparts in TV and the press are totally out of step with the general population in terms of morals. For example, 97 percent believe that a woman has the right to decide if she is going to have an abortion. Moreover, four out of five do not view homosexual relations as wrong. Eighty-six percent support the right of a homosexual to teach in public schools, and 51 percent refuse to condemn adultery as wrong. Only 17 percent strongly agree that extramarital affairs are wrong.[54]

As the researchers observe, "From this evidence, it would be difficult to overestimate the clash of values when television's creative community confronts fundamentalist Christian critics like the Moral Majority or the Coalition for Better Television."[55]

The Hollywood Elite as "Change Agents"

Hollywood's writers, directors, and producers view themselves as crusaders for social reform in America. They see it as their duty to restructure our culture into *their image*. And their image is a humanistic society, devoid of values and free from what they consider the stifling morality of Christianity.

The researchers discovered that two out of three interviewed believe that television entertainment ". . . should be a major force for social reform. This is perhaps the single most striking finding in our study. According to television's creators, they are not in it just for the money. They also seek to move their audience toward their own vision of the good society."[56]

That last statement is worth restating: These Hollywood elitists are not just in the entertainment business for the money—they are evangelists for the religion of humanism. They are actively, consciously, and aggressively using movies and television to turn this nation into a humanistic "Utopia."

Most people are not aware of the ideological practices of Hollywood and its stars, but some illustrations have come to light. Burt Lancaster, for example, was reported to have turned down the role of Moses in *The Ten Commandments,* but he willingly accepted the role of Elmer Gantry, an open ridicule of Christianity and preachers of the Gospel. Later, when Norman Lear launched a TV special to raise funds for his new antichristian organization called "People for the American Way," who do you think served as narrator? Burt Lancaster! This vicious attack on Christianity and its preachers gave him another opportunity to use the media to get his message across.

Jerry Falwell, Pat Robertson, Jim Kennedy, Jim Bakker, and others on Christian television and in films recognize this medium as the world's most powerful vehicle to the minds of people. But their numbers are small compared to Hollywood, their programming providing only one-fourth of the TV fare for the American people. However, research indicates that 22 million people watch religious programs every week.

At least Christian programmers honestly admit their whole motivation is to preach the Christian Gospel. The Hollywood crowd is much less candid. When pressed on using film or television to communicate their left-wing antifamily and often antichristian bias, they say, "We are just being realistic." Nonsense! If the perverted fantasies and anti-conservative doctrine that masquerades as Entertainment City out in Hollywood were the reality of the American people, this nation would already be a defenseless socialist state controlled by Soviet Russia.

It is not surprising, then, that these elitists hate Christians. In their eyes we are the only enemy standing between them and the creation of their new world order. In their warped view of reality, the only real sin is to be a believer in Jesus Christ. Once we can fully grasp who the Hollywood elite are and what they believe in, everything we see on television and in the movies begins to make sense.

In pushing their religion of humanism on us, they try to demonstrate that divorce is fine; premarital sex is natural; adultery is acceptable; drug use is no worse a habit than drinking; homosexual relations are "alternate life-styles"; nuclear power will destroy America; the American military establishment is fascist; Christians are either fools, liars, embezzlers, hypocrites, or secret Nazis; man's life on earth is meaningless; ultraviolence is permissible as long as it is not "gratuitous"; and there are no heroes.

They communicate *their* view of reality each day in countless situation comedies, dramas, and movies. It is a false view of life—a view based upon Satan's lies. But tragically millions of Americans, including Christians, attend their sick movies and spend hours watching silly humanistic programs provided by men whose philosophy is bankrupt and whose morality is often perverse.

Is There Hope for Hollywood?

Can Hollywood ever be redeemed from its degradation? From our limited human perspective, it is hopeless. With God, however, all things are possible. Hollywood needs our prayers—our fervent, consistent prayers. We should pray that God's Spirit will penetrate the Hollywood cesspool in a mighty way!

We should pray that the actors, actresses, producers, directors, and writers will repent and come to Jesus Christ. Satan has held Hollywood captive too long. Perhaps it is time that we Christians launched a spiritual assault on the movie industry to release it from satanic bondage. Why not choose a particular Hollywood personality and begin praying regularly for him?

But we can do even more. Stop supporting the movie industry! Stop watching humanistic propaganda on TV; *boycott* the sponsors of obscene programming. In addition, let the sponsors know how you feel.

Just remember what a few determined people accomplished back in the 1930s when Hollywood was producing pornography. After concerned citizens protested loudly, the Motion Picture Production Code was eventually formed—a code that protected us from filthy movies for over thirty years! Why can't we do it again? If we put enough pressure on the movie and TV industry, they will have to change or suffer enormous losses.

I am convinced that movie producers can make just as much money providing wholesome entertainment as they can by spewing forth trashy films. *Star Wars* and its successors, for example, have been all-time box-office hits. *Raiders of the Lost Ark* is another example that comes to mind. And *Chariots of Fire* was certainly a financial success. Not one of these movies glorified sexual immorality or drug use. We must let the industry realize that we will not tolerate their pornography any longer.

By combining action with prayer, we can bring about a positive change in the movie and TV industry. Hollywood does not have to remain a cesspool. It can be turned into a spring of pure water, producing movies that proclaim the God-given dignity of man and offer hope for the future as they uphold sound Judeo-Christian values. It *is* possible, for with God, *all things are possible,* but it will take a miracle and a national revival.

Christian Television

Norman Lear, a television producer who has used the airwaves for years to peddle his humanist propaganda, is worried about Christians using television to spread the Gospel message. According to Lear, "The ability of the moral majoritarians to shape public debate is unprecedented and poses an enormous danger." Lear advises that the moral majoritarians "have overpowered America's airwaves with their messages of hostility, fear and distrust."[1]

The oft-quoted liberal church historian Martin Marty has warned that Christian television evangelism "threatens to replace the living congregation with a far-flung clientele of devotees to this or that evangelist. This invisible religion is—or ought to be—the most feared contemporary rival to church religion."[2]

The views of Norman Lear and Martin Marty are grossly incorrect, of course. Lear is apprehensive about Christian television because the so-called Religious Right has been effectively using it not only to spread the Gospel but to arouse Christians to take an active role in combating the spread of godless humanism throughout our nation. Lear and his humanist cronies are afraid that a national revival might break out.

And far from undermining the traditional church, as Marty contends, the electronic church serves to inspire and supplement local church activities. As pastor Howard Jones so wisely observed in an issue of *Religious Broadcasting,* "Unless more churches catch the vision for using the media in their evangelistic outreach, we cannot hope to effectively evangelize the world for Christ and hasten His return." Jones added, "Some people object to the churches' use of electronic media. They consider it a threat to the local churches since it draws people away from the houses of worship. I disagree. The electronic church rather complements the ministry of churches, and helps to stimulate growth in them."[3]

Jerry Falwell has been *both* the pastor of a local church and director of a major television ministry. In his opinion, using "the media for the propagation of the Gospel is utilizing the media to its greatest potential. It is an indictment against the church that we have allowed industry to monopolize the media almost totally."[4]

The Beginnings of the Electronic Church

Many evangelists in the 1930s and 1940s recognized the importance of using radio as a means of spreading the Gospel. Men like Charles E. Fuller, M. R. DeHaan, Paul Rader, Percy Crawford, and others pioneered radio evangelism.[5] Charles Fuller's preaching, for example, lead to the conversion of an eighteen-year-old named Jerry Falwell.

Percy Crawford ventured into radio evangelism over FM radio in the 1950s. In 1960 he expanded to UHF television in Philadelphia. His endeavors failed, however, because so few people had UHF TVs at the time.

During the 1950s, men like Oral Roberts and Rex Humbard went on television, paving the way for such future "televangelists" as Jerry Falwell, Pat Robertson, Jim Bakker, Paul Crouch, Charles Stanley, Jim Kennedy, and others.[6]

Thousands of churches across America rent time on a local television station to telecast their morning worship services. Through the medium of TV, virtually every citizen of this country who wants to hear the Gospel on Sunday morning can do so, right in his own home.

Martin Marty and others of his theological stripe castigate the Electric Church, deploring its harmful effect on church growth. He suggests that it substitutes for church attendance and siphons off money that could have been better given to local churches. Nonsense! The facts of church growth during the past thirty years belie his assumption. Televangelism is only thirty-five years old, and church growth in America has been greater during the past thirty years than at any time in history.

Christian Television Adds to the Church

Marty and his liberal cohorts fail to realize that liberalism, not television, is dealing a death blow to their churches. Bible-believing churches are booming today because they offer the converts of television evangelism a place to grow spiritually by teaching the Word of God, plus offering fellowship with other Christians. The liberals' day has passed; people hunger for the reality of God's truth, especially TV converts. So they reject the outdated emptiness of the liberal churches.

Dr. Jerry Falwell has been America's TV pastor for over twenty years, sending more than half a million converts into Bible-teaching churches across the country. I consider Jerry the most influential pastor in the nation. It is no accident that he was recently voted second only to our president as the most admired man in the nation. He estimates that over 30,000 souls a year accept Christ through his "Old Time Gospel" telecast.

During the media's most vicious attack on Jerry Falwell and the Moral Majority leaders, I was interviewed by a Jewish reporter. After the interview was over, I told him how much we Christians loved the Jews and then added, "Off the record, I'd like to ask you a personal question. Have you ever invited Jesus Christ into your life?" He replied, "You sound like a boyhood friend of mine who became a Christian three years ago and is now in seminary studying to become a minister." When I asked how he received Christ, he grinned and said, "Watching Jerry Falwell on television."

When Pat Robertson celebrated his twentieth anniversary on television, he interviewed a woman who, instead of committing suicide, had been converted through watching his program. Then she introduced her best friend, who had also prayed to receive Christ. Their pastor, shown standing in front of his church, stated to the television audience, "Through the testimony of these women, I have baptized and taken into membership one hundred sixty-seven people."

Does that sound as if television hurts the church? No, the smoke-screen argument to discredit the use of the most powerful vehicle ever invented to win people to Christ evaporates upon close scrutiny. After pastoring one of America's great churches for twenty-five years, I would not have resigned to dedicate the rest of my life to ministering to families through television if I were not convinced that it is today's most powerful tool for reaching people for Christ *and* adding to His church. I am convinced that unless the liberals regain control of our federal government in future elections, enabling them to cut off the use of the airwaves for Christian television preaching and teaching, we have only begun to see the use of this powerful medium by the church of Jesus Christ.

The Christian Broadcasting Network

In 1959 Pat Robertson, a Yale lawyer and recently ordained Southern Baptist minister, packed up his family and moved to Portsmouth, Virginia, from the Bedford-Stuyvesant section of Brooklyn. The Lord had given him the vision of purchasing a run-down UHF TV station in Portsmouth. At the time he knew absolutely nothing about television; in fact, he didn't even own a set. But he drove into Portsmouth with seventy dollars in his pocket and quickly negotiated the purchase of the station for $37,000. He lacked funds but possessed a tremendous faith that God would supply every need.

In 1962 Pat Robertson went on the air with the nation's first Christian broadcasting network. He was the pioneer of Christian television and still pushes ahead of the rest with innovative—and sometimes controversial—programming. Robertson has an enormous drive to reach America with God's message. His friend and biographer Jamie Buckingham has said, "... It is this drive to compete with the very best—despite a few failures—which has pushed CBN to the top. Robertson has long believed in professional excellence."[7]

Today the CBN Cable Network is the nation's second-largest cable TV programming service and is by far the largest religious network, carried on over 3,500 cable systems, reaching nearly 20 million subscribers. According to a Nielsen survey, 6.5 million households watch CBN each day.[8] CBN has commercial stations in Atlanta, Dallas, Boston, and Norfolk.

Pat is wisely trying to make the breakthrough into commercial sponsorship of Christian programming. Somehow we have to wake up Christian businessmen and other pro-moral advertisers to start advertising on Christian television. If the networks can charge billions of dollars to subsidize Norman Lear and Lee Rich's brand of immoral programming, why can't those committed to Christ and traditional moral values subsidize through their business those programs that will help return this nation to moral sanity?

By the time you read this book, I hope to have secured sponsors for our thirty-minute program, "The LaHayes on Family Life." It is just a matter of time before some businessmen realize the advantage of aiming their advertising dollars at the 69 million born-again people out there who buy cars, TV sets, clothes, and food. When that happens, we will no longer have to ask for donations to get our message out, for the free-enterprise system itself will advance the Kingdom of God and turn America around. Commercial advertising of selected Christian programming is one way for businessmen to use the free-enterprise system to save the system. At present large business corporations subsidize their own destruction by advertising on shows that are antibusiness and anti-free enterprise. That's like paying thieves to rob my home! Someday Proctor and Gamble, General Mills, and the hundred other major industries in this country will redirect their advertising dollars into more viable channels.

Jim Bakker and the PTL Cable Network

Jim Bakker is another innovator in Christian television. He and his wife, Tammy, began working in Christian TV with CBN over eighteen years ago, producing a children's puppet show. Bakker, who pioneered the format of "The 700 Club," was Pat Robertson's cohost for nearly eight years.[9]

Bakker and his wife left CBN, spending time in California before finally settling in Charlotte, North Carolina. In 1974 he launched the daily "Jim Bakker" show, and PTL television network became a reality. Today PTL, a cable network, appears on 220 stations and carries a viewing audience estimated at 2.4 million. It provides twenty-four-hour-a-day Christian programming.

In addition Bakker has created foreign versions of his program, using nationals as hosts in France, Spain, Thailand, Japan, Africa, and elsewhere. These shows are all produced overseas.

Paul Crouch and the Trinity Broadcasting Network

Paul Crouch is president and founder of the Trinity Broadcasting Network, headquartered in Tustin, California. Starting with one station in southern California in 1973, the TBN network is now linked to over 250 cable systems and the six UHF stations owned and operated by the ministry. At this writing, Crouch is negotiating for the purchase of a seventh TV station in Seattle.

TBN has specialized in the production of Christian programs. At present, as many as eighty different ministries use TBN facilities to produce weekly Christian programs. These shows are produced not only in southern California, but in Phoenix, Oklahoma City, and Miami.

Using satellite technology, TBN distributes Christian programming twenty-four hours a day.[10]

Programming for Every Need

Through these three major Christian television cable networks, Christian programming is conveyed in basically eight different ways: Christian specials, traditional church services, musicals, fund raising through prime-time specials and telethons, talk shows, TV spots (short vignettes between regular programming), drama, and prime-time secular television shows containing Christian values.[11]

Every Christian program on the air falls into one of these categories, and each program can and does minister to the needs of a particular segment of the viewing audience. Remember, God loves variety. He made each of us unique, with different tastes and needs. Just as there are many churches to meet particular individual needs, so there are different Christian television programs fulfilling the various needs of the viewers. As Paul points out in Ephesians 4:11–14, the Christian church has a multifaceted function in our world. The electronic church must try to minister to the varied needs of believers *and* reach out to the lost.

In our weekly television program, "The LaHayes on Family Life," my wife, Bev, and I do not attempt to replicate a church service. There is certainly a place for television church services, but we feel constrained to create nonchurchy, down-to-earth, practical programs that supply Bible answers for twentieth-century man and his family. Even though our primary burden is not soul winning, we have seen many individuals come to Christ who wouldn't watch a church service but value the family life theme and yet receive a strong Christian message. No one program will meet the needs or satisfy the tastes of everyone. But through a diversity of programs we can all have a part in ministering to the 227 million souls that make up this country.

Christian Television Isn't Perfect!

Television evangelists do not always accomplish their lofty goals, and some have made mistakes in this new and complex industry. In addition, some phonies may take part in the Electronic Church, just as in any field. But as Jerry Falwell has so wisely commented, "God has given us gifts today to reach the world, and He has ordered that we use those gifts for His glory. I will not put the gift of the broadcast media aside because there are charlatans and phonies in Christendom."[12] Having met most of today's major programmers, I am happy to say that the majority of them are sincere ministers of the Word with a deep burden to reach the lost.

Some justifiable criticisms have been leveled against Christian television in America, and at times we encounter excesses. But what we have in this country far surpasses what is being accomplished in other nations of the world. Maurice Rowlandson, an evangelist in Great Britain, is generally pleased with American Christian television. He observes, "You have the freedom in the United States to tune into something that you would like to listen to or watch. You've got Heinz 57 variety here. Now in Britain you haven't got the freedom to do that. You only have the freedom to watch and listen to what you are *told* you ought to, but not what *you* want to."[13]

Myra Grant, assistant professor of broadcast writing in the Communications Center at Wheaton Graduate School, has noted, "Evangelicals and Christians of many different denominations have understood the importance of media and the potential of media both for teaching and even for evangelizing. However, many mistakes have been made, but at least, they were on the battlefield and struggling and interacting and trying to contend with the technology and the culture of the industry."[14]

In a field as relatively new as Christian television, mistakes are bound to be made. In any field innovation is dangerous. Men like Pat Robertson, Jim Bakker, Paul Crouch, and others have lead the way in harnessing satellite communications technology for the spreading of the Gospel message around the world. They have probably blundered numerous times along the way, and their cynical critics have attacked them mercilessly. The great evangelist D. L. Moody likewise suffered from such criticism. Cynics would ignore his message or pick at his grammatical errors and preaching style. But as he repeatedly replied to his critics, "I like my way of doing things better than your way of *not* doing them."

Fund-Raising Techniques in Christian Television

Undoubtedly one of the biggest criticisms of Christian television today involves the area of fund raising, especially raising support through direct mail (so-called junk mail). Pastors of local churches have come down on the televangelists for supposedly draining support from their churches. Other critics have correctly observed that some charlatans take advantage of helpless widows who survive on Social Security checks. By using crude psychological manipulation, some electronic church ministers are accused of using their audiences for personal gain.

Money—how it is raised and used—has always been a hot issue. But we have allowed the secular media to blow the few excesses in TV fund raising well out of proportion. They have made sincere attempts to fund very expensive means of communicating the Word of God seem ugly and disreputable when, in most cases, it has been done quite responsibly and ethically.

The hypocrisy of the media appears, however, in the contrast between their attack on electronic church evangelists and their amazing silence (which suggests tacit approval) with regard to porno producers. How many times have we heard or read about the "$1 billion a year the electronic church raises each year"? But when did we ever hear the self-appointed guardians of ethics use their media outlets to complain about the *$6 billion* raised last year by the pornography business?

Why is it permissible for porno producers to corrupt the minds and morals of a nation, graphically increase the rate of forceable rape, and greatly accelerate the growing problems of child molestation and incest in the procuring of their $6 billion but wrong for us to raise $1 billion? (Keep in mind, almost 50 percent of what we raise goes to pay air time and production costs, 25–35 percent supports the fund-raising process, and the rest is needed to pay the salaries of those who work in the ministry.) The answer is: ideology! The Hefners, Flynts, and Gucciones may profane the name of God and disgrace womanhood, femininity, and decency as long as they keep prattling their liberal/humanist philosophy. But TV evangelists are condemned not for the $1 billion they raise each year, but because they advocate a return to moral sanity. The money question is just a smokescreen. Always keep in mind that today's media consistently protect their fellow liberal brothers, whether in politics, media, education, or entertainment. And they just as consistently attack conservatives, wherever they appear. They label their attacks objective reporting, of course.

Why They Ask for Money

Almost everyone asks the question, Why do these godly ministers use airtime to ask for money? When my wife and I inaugurated our family-life program, we were such idealists that we pledged not to ask for money on the air or write "train-wreck fund-raising letters." That sounded good, but one thing was wrong: It didn't work.

During my thirty years in the ministry, I have pastored three churches and either founded or helped to start eleven different church organizations. Without question, the hardest task I have ever undertaken is trying to start a national TV ministry! Television absorbs money the way quicksand consumes a victim. In one month alone we lost $71,000. Talk about pressure! In fact, it was just such an experience that inspired me to write *How to Manage Your Pressures Before They Manage You.*

Televangelists and radio evangelists ask for money and send out fund appeals because it is necessary. Until we can awaken Christian businessmen to advertise on certain Christian programs as a legitimate business expense, as a means of promoting their products in the Christian marketplace, and as a strategy for advancing the Kingdom, there is no alternative. My wife and I have traveled to over 195 cities during an eighteen-month period, holding fund-raising banquets or one-night family life mini-seminars to find supporters for our TV program. That isn't a regimen I would wish on anyone!

Fund-Raising Letters Are Scriptural

One of my friends in a media ministry is often teased by his minister friends for his frequent fund-raising appeals. At one meeting where we were both speaking, the master of ceremonies introduced him with the humorous story that one of his church members approved his methods because, since his wife died, the minister is the only one who writes to him every day. Another friend reportedly sent him a check for $1,000 with the message, "I have joined every club and supported every new project you have started. The first $500 of this check is for your present fund-raising project; the other $500 is for the next one you start."

All who receive direct-mail solicitation are not inclined to appreciate such humor. Sometimes the fund raiser is too intense, and sometimes the recipient doesn't realize that fund-raising letters originated with the apostle Paul. In 1 Corinthians 16:1, 2, for example, Paul tells his readers, "Now concerning what you wrote about the money to be raised to help God's people in Judea. You must do what I told the churches in Galatia to do. Every Sunday each of you must put aside some money, in proportion to what he has earned, and save it up, so there will be no need to collect money when I come." He also attempted to raise support for poverty-stricken believers in 2 Corinthians 8.

In addition, Philippians 4:15–17, he says, "You Philippians know very well that when I left Macedonia in the early days of preaching the Good News, you were the only church to help me; you were the only ones who shared my profits and losses. More than once when I needed help in Thessalonica, you sent it to me. It is not that I just want to receive gifts; rather, I want to see profit added to your account."

If Paul approved the technique of writing churches in order to raise support (and remember, he was soliciting funds for his itinerant ministry *outside* the local church), I certainly consider fund-raising letters a valid means of obtaining support for a ministry that reaches out to an estimated 22 million people every week.

I would have to agree with televangelist Jimmy Swaggart, who has written, "Any outreach effort has to have *money* to run its operations. Every church receives from one to 10 offerings in a week. Appeals are made from the pulpit urging church members to give. There's nothing wrong with this, if done with taste and propriety. By the same token, there's nothing wrong with the television preacher making appeals for contributions, either by letter or through television. But it is the manner in which this is done that we are discussing."[15]

America Needs a Fourth Network

I have long believed that America surely needs a fourth television network to compete with the media monopolists at ABC, NBC, and CBS. I know that both Pat Robertson and Ted Turner have had similar visions. It appears as if Turner may be getting close to establishing a fourth network or buying one of the major networks. I could not predict what he might do if he did gain control of a network, for when my wife and I talked to him in his office about carrying our program on his network, he made it clear that he was not a Christian and did not agree with some of our pro-moral commitments. He has, however, gone on public record as opposing the three networks for their anti-moral programming that is having a very harmful effect on the families of America. If he gained control of one of the big three networks, he would probably improve the programming to an acceptable family level. I doubt that he would modify the flaming liberal fare of the news-gathering force, however. His present CNN news force is only slightly less liberal than that of his network competition.

I have felt that conservatives and Christians should pool their resources to create a fourth network. An enormous market of viewers out there can certainly support a commercially sponsored network dedicated to providing wholesome family entertainment. The majority of the people in America do not enjoy watching the mindless drivel disseminated by the major networks. They tend to reject programs that push homosexuality, infidelity, or violence. Actually, the television *viewing audience* is comprised of only *half* the population of America. That's right—only half of our population watches television. So when we read that a terribly immoral show such as "Dallas" has a rating of 25 percent, remember that the statistic represents 25 percent of the *viewing audience,* not the entire population. A minority of the people in this country can make "Dallas" a hit. But what about the rest of us who desire wholesome programming? We don't count.

Many knowledgeable Americans believe that if some Christian and conservative businessmen pooled their resources and bought one network, they could turn a handsome profit. By producing only wholesome family-quality programs and advancing a conservative view of the news, they would attract a greater audience than any of the liberal-dominated networks. In addition, they would rekindle the viewing habits of the millions who have become so disillusioned with TV that they have just shut it off. The cost? about $900 million!

Admittedly, that is a high price, but if something isn't done soon to provide the American people with an alternative to the liberal brainwashing of the existing networks, the media may so condition the voters to elect pro-Socialist liberals to office that Americans will forfeit both their national freedom and the free-enterprise system. As one wealthy man warned, "If we don't use corporate profits to buy a network to balance the view presented to the American people, we will soon lose our corporations." When enough men with means recognize this important fact, they will buy and operate a network helping to turn this country back to freedom. I just hope they wake up in time!

What Is the Future for Television?

If the last ten years are any indication of where TV is going in the future, and I believe it is, you can expect several very significant changes in television broadcasting in just the next five years.

1. The Three Networks Will Become Even More Secular! Those who control ABC, CBS, NBC, and the public broadcasting networks have shown by their programs over the years that they hate the Gospel of Jesus Christ. They long for the day they can find other buyers for Sunday morning time than religious programmers. The *only* reason Jerry Falwell, Pat Robertson, Jim Bakker, and others have been able to rent the time on these stations is because the networks couldn't get other buyers to pay the same price. Gradually, however, they are inventing programming that will banish religion from the airwaves—even on Sunday. Recently, our thirty-minute weekly program was bumped from our local CBS affiliate for "CBS Sunday Mornings." Two years ago they couldn't find anyone to pay advertising time for 8:30 A.M., Sundays. Now they have learned that a news-hungry nation will pay for it. And they want to charge us the same rate for 7:00 A.M., when most people are still asleep, as we used to pay for 8:30 A.M.

I predict that in five years all religious programs will be off the three networks! (or banished to the unearthly hour of 6:00 A.M., for the same price). Since PBS, the Public Broadcasting Network, already discriminates against religious programs, that will mean total secularization of the four most powerful networks in North America—at least by the end of the eighties and perhaps sooner.

2. The Networks Will Become Sexier. As they drive religious programs off "their networks," the secularists will pander even more to the prurient interest and drop to all-time-low moral standards. By charting the moral decline of their programming during the past decade, we can project at the same rate what it will be by the mid-nineties and beyond—fare that is fit only for citizens of Sodom and Gomorrah.

The networks have already learned that 15 to 20 percent of the TV viewers enjoy smut, filth, and sexually shocking fare. Another 20 to 30 percent are such TV addicts they put up with moral standards unfit for the back alley just so they can enjoy "free entertainment." These two groups provide them the viewing base they need to charge advertisers millions of dollars. What happens to the other 50 percent of the nation's viewers? Except for sports, news, and carefully selected specials, they shut it off. TV programming in the late eighties and early nineties will increasingly appeal to moral perverts—and turn off increasing millions of pro-moral viewers.

3. *Cable Television—the Wave of the Future.* Ted Turner of TBS, Pat Robertson of CBN, and other pioneers of cable television will eventually fill the void for those who prefer an alternative. Currently about 40 percent of the nation is on cable and hopefully by 1990, 85 percent of our homes will have that capability. Unfortunately, it brings with it HBO and pornography beyond reason. As long as the ACLU and secular humanists can club the FCC and Supreme Court with their excessive views of free speech and free press under the First Amendment, such filth peddlers will be protected. Hopefully, future legislators will be raised up who oppose such abuse of the public airwaves and put a stop to it.

Currently, the Southern Baptists are launching a new network for their 14 million members, called *ACTS*. It will combine cable, UHF, and perhaps low-power-frequency capabilities when it is authorized. They plan a variety of family programming according to the standards and values of their denomination and look on it as a powerful tool for evangelism. With the low moral fare being pumped out by the networks, I think they may find millions of non-Christian families who prefer wholesome programs, who will join them as viewers. I would think that such pro-family-type viewers would be good candidates for the Gospel.

4. *Direct Broadcast Satellite Technology.* The Dominion Satellite Network, headed by Robert W. Johnson of Naples, Florida, will launch in 1984, a unique result of advancing technology. Called "an angel in the sky," he is buying time on a space satellite that will permit them continuous broadcasting for both television and radio. According to Johnson, "Nationwide research shows there is an audience large enough to attract national advertisers for wholesome family programming that upholds Judeo-Christian ethics, and that's what ours will do."[16] When operational in 1985–1986, it may just spread like wildfire.

Families who desire a wholesome alternative to current fare can purchase a small receiving dish to put on their roofs and pull in the kind of programming, religious, news, sports, and education that can be of positive value. It is estimated that 1 million subscribers will join this outlet the first year. Canadian Christians who do not have access to cable TV will particularly appreciate this new feature.

Anyone interested in more information on how you can pull in three wholesome pro-family TV channels and at least three similar radio stations with one antenna, just send a self-addressed stamped envelope to me, P.O. Box 16000, San Diego, CA 92116, for free information.

Can We Help Christian Television?

As individuals, we can do much to aid the various television ministries in America. We can certainly pray for them, and we can give financial support to our favorite TV ministries as well.

If you are displeased with what you see on television, whether Christian or secular, let the programmers know. But don't waste time writing to the networks, complaining about the immoral fare they offer. Remember, they do it because that is the way they think. The only way to get their attention is to hit them in the pocketbook. Since they receive their money from advertisers, write to the sponsors of objectionable shows. If enough people complain to the 100 major TV sponsors and threaten *not* to buy their products if they continue to advertise such antifamily programs, they will order the networks to halt their flow of morally perverse programming.

You can also address your objections to the FCC. If millions of citizens would express their discontent regarding the present abuses of the government-controlled airwaves, the media would be given a federal order to clean up their act. The FCC address is 1919 M Street, N.W., Washington, D.C. 20554.

Whenever you see a product sponsoring a Christian program, tell the merchant when you go to the store how much you appreciate what he is doing and try to patronize his business. If 69 million Christians would boycott those who sponsor filthy programs and purchase from those who advertise on Christian programming, we would soon see new programs on our airwaves.

At thirty-five years of age, television is still a developing medium. Hopefully it will mature into responsible programming. Christian television, much younger and still attempting to toddle without stumbling, needs our support, not our censure. It may yet make even greater breakthroughs and one day provide every home in this country with wholesome profamily fare and free communication of the Word of God.

I believe that if the apostle Paul were alive today, he would be using TV to reach the world with the Gospel. And he might even ask for money to support his programs.

Cable Television: Friend or Foe?

Cable television has been around almost as long as commercial television. In fact, it began in the hills of Oregon and Pennsylvania, back in the late 1940s, just as television sets were beginning to be mass marketed to an eager public.

Cable television was once called Community Antenna Television (CATV). In mountainous areas, TV viewers found it almost impossible to receive the signals from distant commercial stations. So enterprising businessmen built a huge master antenna on the top of the mountain to receive the signal. They then ran wires (or cables) from their master antenna down into the community and sold the service to local subscribers for a monthly fee. That's how cable television first got its start.

But although cable TV has been available for over thirty years, it never became truly profitable until the Federal Communications Commission gradually removed restrictions on it, beginning in the 1970s.

The FCC had been reluctant to allow the cable industry to compete on an equal footing with the major networks, apparently fearing that the competition would upset the nation's communications system. In fact, in 1966 the FCC issued its "Second Order and Report" on cable television. This report effectively kept the cable operators out of the top 100 television markets in America, which consisted of nearly 85 percent of the households in America.[1]

FCC policies have changed in recent years. In March of 1972, the

FCC issued guidelines that have revolutionized the cable industry. These stipulated that cable operators *could* enter the top 100 markets in America if they guaranteed to provide at least twenty channels and the following services: locally originated programming, leased channels for pay TV and similar services, uncensored public access to a cable channel, a channel for educational programs, a channel for municipal services, and a capacity for two-way interactive communication between the viewer and the television production being aired.[2]

Cable TV: The Wave of the Future?

Communications experts view cable television as the wave of the future in America's rapid video revolution. The expansion of the industry in just over ten years has been phenomenal. In 1974 cable television reached into 12 percent of the households in America; today the A. C. Nielsen Company estimates that over 40 percent of the homes in America are now wired for cable.[3] And Ted Turner, one of the greatest innovators in the cable-TV industry, predicts that 52 percent of the homes in America will be wired by January 1, 1985. By the end of the century, 85 to 90 percent of all homes will have cable.

Cable television is looked upon by communications researchers as more than simply a vehicle for additional entertainment programming. It is considered a revolutionary communications system—a system that might someday actually have every household in America linked together electronically to each other and to government agencies and businesses.

We may eventually be able to do our banking using a computer terminal attached to our cable television system, shop by TV just by pressing a button to order what appears on the screen, participate in political polls, and have access to hundreds of data banks throughout the United States and the world. Cable television, hooked up to a printer, may provide us with our magazines, newspaper, and even mail service. It may also allow an employee to work at home, performing all his tasks in the comfort of his own abode, rather than traveling to the office.

These are just a few of the many possibilities of cable television. Of course, the most significant application of cable technology at this point lies in the provision of a wide variety of additional choices for American viewers.

I am somewhat dubious about the value of added television shows for viewers, but cable TV may at least perform an invaluable service: By drawing more and more viewers away from the three monopolistic networks, it may actually help break the stranglehold of those networks on our communications system. If cable TV can undermine the economic base of the giant monopolies, they might come tumbling down. The destruction of ABC, NBC, and CBS would probably be one of the most beneficial events in our nation in a long, long time.

Cable Television Is Having Its Own Problems

During the last few years, the bright future predicted for cable television has dimmed somewhat. Many factors are involved—most of them related to money and greed.

Because cable TV does not broadcast over the public airwaves, it has been subjected to fewer restrictions by the FCC than regular commercial stations. Its signals travel through privately owned cables, into subscribers' homes. States and local governments are charged with controlling cable television through the issuance of local franchise licenses. Bidding for these franchises has become one of the major obstacles facing the cable operators in recent years. In their zeal, city officials often make unreasonable demands upon the cable companies competing for a franchise.

Some cable systems simply drop out. American Television & Communications Corp, a subsidiary of Time, Inc., has recently stopped bidding on big-city franchises. According to president Trygve E. Myhren, ". . . We looked at the crazy demands of the cities, the political opportunism, and the eagerness of cable operators to win at almost any price, and decided there was no way to make the risks pay off."[4]

The cost of installing a cable system in a big city can run as high as $1,200 per subscriber—up to $300 million per city. Many systems take as many as five years to complete and will not even show a profit for ten years.[5] Yet many city governments seem intent on gouging cable operators for as much of the profit as they can get. Boston, for example, wanted 8 percent of the annual revenues, yet offered to impose a subscriber fee of only $2.00. And the cable company that won the Sacramento, California, franchise had to promise $90 million in construction projects, local studios, and job-training programs.[6]

After the cable companies install their systems, they are faced with another problem: dropouts. Of all who subscribe to cable, between 28 percent and 35 percent of them cancel within a year. The cost of wiring a home and then having to disconnect it within a year seriously erodes any profits a company might hope to make.

Another problem facing some older cable companies concerns expiring contracts. Some cities, instead of automatically renewing the franchise, reopen the bidding to get a better deal with newer cable systems.

One final difficulty has arisen: Several lawsuits are pending, which challenge the right of a cable company to maintain its monopoly in a community. The cable companies argue that the exorbitant costs necessary to wire cities must translate into monopolies so they can make a profit. Phoenix, however, is allowing two cable companies to wire the city. What will happen when both begin competing for customers is anyone's guess.

Higher Copyright Fees Jeopardize Cable Systems

Until 1976, cable operators could retransmit the signals from commercial stations into distant communities without paying any kind of fee for the use of the programming. For years Hollywood producers and broadcasters have been complaining that cable companies have been, in effect, pirating their expensive productions from commercial stations without having to pay royalty fees.

All this changed, however, in 1976 when the copyright law was rewritten. In the new law, a fixed royalty fee for cable operators was established. A Copyright Royalty Tribunal was instituted to oversee the payment of these royalties to the motion picture industry, television syndicators, music groups, and others.

Under the most recent adjustments in this fee schedule, a cable system will have to pay 3.75 percent of its gross revenues if it rebroadcasts programming from stations located from thirty-five to forty miles away. Cable operators claim that the new fee will force them to drop several of the "super stations"—those who broadcast via satellite. Thus 6 million cable subscribers may lose Ted Turner's WTBS, WOR-TV in New York, and WGN-TV in Chicago.[7] For what will be a sevenfold increase in royalty payments, the cable companies will choose to drop these stations rather than pay.

Cable Pornography and "Public Access"

When the FCC more heavily regulated the cable industry, one of its guidelines for allowing cable into the 100 top markets was that the cable systems had to maintain uncensored public access to a cable channel. The FCC decided that minority and social groups could use this new technology to create innovative programs for local viewing.

In some communities this has happened with great success. The city of Atlanta, for example, has a public-access station featuring five neighborhood studios. Nearly 2,000 local residents have been trained to use these facilities, and various community groups have produced arts-and-crafts shows, news programs, and productions for children and senior citizens.

Public-access programming has also benefited the citizens of Bloomington, Indiana. Don R. Smith, manager of the Community Access Channel, reports, "There are lots of groups putting out quality community programming in this country." His station was created in 1974 with partial funding from the local library. Private citizens groups produce local news programs, live election coverage, documentaries, and cultural programs.[8]

Unfortunately, the kooks and the pornographers have also gained public access to the cable systems. The worst offenders seem to be in New York, where two cable systems have split the Manhattan market: Group W Cable and Manhattan Cable. Their combined coverage is 350,000 subscribers.[9] Both cable companies have been victimized by lunatics and sexual degenerates. One young man used the cable system to show a videotape of him shooting his dog. Al Goldstein, editor of *Screw* magazine, produces "Midnight Blue," featuring wet T-shirt contests, nude dancing, movies vividly portraying brutal rapes, and tours through weird sex clubs. Still another feature is "The Robyn Byrd Show." A blonde stripper disco dances, does exercises, and takes phone calls from men who fantasize about her.[10]

Public access, as we have seen, can benefit a community. However, it can also provide an outlet for the most obscene pornography imaginable.

We Can Eliminate Cableporn

Many people are under the mistaken impression that pornography cannot be removed from our televisions because of First Amendment protections. But that's simply not true. Already sufficient laws exist in our communities and at state and federal levels to keep all pornographic materials off TV. However, these laws are not being enforced. Why? Because law-enforcement offices will not prosecute pornographers unless the public is sufficiently aroused to pressure them into taking action.

Numerous communities throughout the country *are* aggressively fighting cable pornography. According to Bruce Taylor, chief counsel for Citizens for Decency Through Law, the city of Milwaukee, Wisconsin, that city has one of the toughest cableporn laws in America. "The city council," explained Taylor, "passed a cable ordinance that requires any cable company that gets the bid to refrain from showing obscene or indecent material, which means that not only can they prohibit it from showing movies like 'Deep Throat' or 'Caligula,' but they're not going to be able to show any nudity at all."[11]

In the spring of 1982, Maurice Ferre, the mayor of Miami began an all-out campaign against cableporn in his community after he had seen New York's public-access channels. Sitting in his New York hotel room late one evening, trying to find a news program, he chanced upon cableporn. As he recalls, "It was a program with a bunch of people totally naked, sitting around talking about sex."[12]

Enraged, he returned to Miami and contacted the two cable companies vying for a franchise. He persuaded them to refrain from showing any pornography until the public could vote on the issue. In a referendum held September 7, 1982, 51.8 percent of the voting public

came out against cableporn. The city commission then drafted a tough
antiporn ordinance to keep cable pornography out of Miami.

"Indecent" Materials Can Be Banned

The Supreme Court has ruled that material shown over television or
broadcast over the radio does not have to be proven legally "obscene"
to be banned. For a film or book or magazine to be declared obscene,
lawyers must determine whether "the average person, applying contemporary community standards, would find that the work, taken as a
whole, appeals to the prurient interest; whether the work depicts or
describes, in a patently offensive way, sexual conduct specifically defined by the applicable state law; and whether the work, taken as a
whole, lacks serious literary, artistic, political, or scientific value." This
is the definition of obscenity as defined by the Supreme Court in the
1973 *Miller* v. *California* decision.[13]

But the Supreme Court has maintained that different standards may
be applied to the broadcasting industry. The court outlined its reason-
ings when it handed down the *FCC* v. *Pacifica Foundation* decision
in 1978. This case involved a lawsuit brought by the FCC against a
Pacifica-owned radio station for broadcasting filthy language in violation of Section 1464 of Title 18 of the United States Code.[14]

In this ruling, the court made it clear that broadcasting is a unique
form of communication and must be regulated in a special way. What
might be reasonably prohibited from radio or television, might not
necessarily be banned in print. The majority observed, ". . . Broadcast
media have established a uniquely pervasive presence in the lives of all
Americans. Patently offensive, indecent material presented over the
airwaves confronts the citizen, not only in public, but also in the privacy of the home, where the individual's right to be left alone plainly
outweighs the First Amendment rights of the intruder."[15]

The court also observed that children need special protection from
the broadcasting of indecent materials. "Broadcasting is uniquely ac-
cessible to children, even those too young to read . . . Other forms of
offensive expression may be withheld from the young without re-
stricting the expression at its source. Bookstores and motion picture
theaters, for example, may be prohibited from making indecent mate-

rials available to children. We held in *Ginzberg* v. *New York* ... [the] government's interest in the 'well-being of its youth' and in supporting 'parents' claim to authority in their own household' justified the regulation of otherwise protected expression."[16]

Cableporn can be eliminated from our TV screens, but only if concerned citizens make their views known. It is foolhardy to enter into a fight against pornographers, however, if you are poorly educated on the issues and lack adequate legal advice. Pornographers hire the best (and most unscrupulous) lawyers in the business. And they have the power of organized crime's millions to back them up. The wise course of action is to contact an organization like Citizens for Decency Through Law to help you fight cableporn in your area. Their address is listed in Appendix A.

Cable Television: Friend or Foe?

That's up to you and me. Cable TV can be overtaken by the liberals, the humanists, and the pornographers to be used for their own evil purposes. On the other hand, dedicated Christians can organize at the local level to use this new technology for positive purposes.

If your community is now served by a cable system, your church or social group has every right to produce programming for local viewing. If you are interested in using the public-access channels to produce wholesome, quality programs to benefit your community, contact your local cable company and find out what you need to do to inaugurate your own program. In many cases, the cable company is required to train you. But do your homework *first.* Your local library may have current information on your city's cable system, including the franchise agreement. Study this material and then get organized.

If your city is not now served by a cable system, do your homework early and aggressively oppose cableporn before it invades your town.

Cable television can become our worst enemy, but only if we sit back and allow liberals, humanists, and pornographers to run it.

What Can We Do About the Media?

If America is going to return to moral sanity, millions of our people must become informed of the issues and organize their efforts to counter the liberal/humanist blitzkreig that has been bombing our nation for half a century. That is why I always include in my books some positive suggestions of what we can do to help.

What We Can Do About the Hidden Censors of the Media

1. Pray for the actors, writers, producers, editors, reporters, and technical personnel involved in our communications media. Pray also for Christians in the secular media. Pick a specific reporter, newscaster, and actor, and so on and begin praying for his or her salvation.

Pray also that a sufficient number of Christians will awaken to the rapid secularization of our country through the liberal domination of our media. Ask God to awaken businessmen to the fact that their advertising dollars promote the destruction of the free-enterprise system by subsidization of the liberal-only philosophy of the media. And pray for a national revival that would make holy living fashionable and, by contrast, expose humanism's amorality.

2. More Christians should get involved in the media. We need to purchase newspapers, magazines, TV and radio stations, and film-production companies. We must supply alternative forms of communication for the majority of the American public.

We have established some fifty Christian TV stations in this country. That means over 110 major markets are not within the reach of Christian programming, except the few times they are available for purchase. Local Christian businessmen in those cities that yet do not have Christian television ought to pool their resources and provide such for their community, whether by UHF, VHF, or low-power frequency such as cable TV.

I will never understand why Christian and conservative businessmen sit back and let the pornography kings buy up the cable TV stations.

3. We need a fourth TV network committed to profamily and conservative programming. It is still a mystery to me why conservative and Christian capitalists fail to realize that the media as presently controlled will soon destroy our free-enterprise system and with it their ability to make money. Surely they must comprehend that the tax-tax, spend-spend practices of government are advocated by the media. "Let government provide," the liberal/socialist philosophy, will soon ruin this country.

We need a coalition of businessmen who will use their corporate profits to buy up one of the existing networks or create another one and dedicate it to wholesome family programming. At least they can create a conservative news-gathering network and offer the other side of the news to the independent, conservative-owned, and Christian stations in order to offset the continual barrage we get from the left-leaning TV towers of NBC, CBS, and ABC.

4. We must actively oppose godless humanism and immorality in the media by letter-writing campaigns and boycotts. Boycott the sponsors of questionable programming. Let the networks and sponsors know how you feel. Boycott immoral films as well, and let the Hollywood studio heads hear your objections.

5. Christians and Christian businessmen *must* do everything they can to support wholesome programs and Christian radio and television efforts.

Christian TV and radio is powerful but expensive. Instead of grumbling about the executive Christian administrators and TV owners always begging for money, believers should realize that they need our support. Without them, the left would be in total control of the most powerful vehicle to the mind in the country.

It is amazing to me that Christians will pay ten dollars or more a month to buy cable TV, yet not give one dime to those who produce the programs they watch. If every Christian family donated as much for Christian television as for cable and the TV set, no Christian program would ever have to ask for money again. In fact we would have more time to program and more money to provide better programs.

During our first two years on TV, I spent 80 percent of my time raising money to spend 20 percent of my time ministering through television, and I have millions of book-ready friends. Just imagine how those who are not authors must struggle to provide a meaningful message as an alternative to the usual humanistic fare.

Christian TV should not be the responsibility of just a few thousand people; it should be shared by the 69 million who, according to Gallup, are born again.

We must urge Congress to investigate the three major networks and break up their monopolistic stranglehold on our public airwaves.

In *The Networks: How They Stole the Show,* A. Frank Reel suggests several ways to do this. One way to break the monopoly would be to simply abolish VHF broadcasting and have all TV stations operate in the UHF band.[1] This would enable ten or twenty new stations to open up in every major city.

Another possible solution is *deintermixture.* Under this concept, stations would be rearranged so that the cities would either have all-UHF or all-VHF stations. Because the networks have gained such a tight control over VHF, this would loosen their hold on many lucrative markets in America.

One of the best possible solutions would be to simply rule that the networks are "common carriers" like our telephone lines. Under this concept, networks would have absolutely no control over programming or content. They would simply sell time to anyone having sufficient funds to air a program.

6. We must vigorously oppose the deregulation of the broadcast industry. Television would degenerate as quickly as the movie industry did when the production code was abolished in 1966. The effect in

Italy provides a good example of what we can expect here if all restraints are removed. In 1976 the Italian government eliminated all restrictions on television programming. As a result the networks began to show hard-core pornography to compete for higher ratings.

Television laissez-faire would not only proliferate pornography on our airwaves, but would possibly feature live suicides on TV. And I'm not joking. A Hollywood producer named Laurence Schwab is actually working on a TV series called "Suicide." He will place a suicide hotline number in phone books, and advertise it on radio and television. When a potential suicide victim calls him, he will contact a psychiatrist to visit the person—along with a camera crew. As Schwab explains it, ". . . We will not egg a person on; our psychiatrist will try to prevent the suicide. But if the person decides that he does not want our counseling, and that he must take his life, my response is: Film it. Show it."[2]

That's the sort of depraved programming we can expect on television if the industry is deregulated.

Now that the left-leaning humanists control the three networks, public broadcasting, and much cable TV, deregulation would be patently unfair, giving them absolute control over the thirty-five-year-old media. It would be akin to signing two boxers to a championship fight, but requiring one to fight with both hands tied behind him and giving the other freedom to strike at will. The outcome would be as predictable as deregulation of the FCC.

As a rock-ribbed conservative, I say the FCC should do more regulating, not less. They should establish a true fairness and morality code, enforcing or canceling existing licenses as necessary.

7. We must oppose cable pornography in our communities. If your community is being threatened by cableporn, contact Citizens for Decency Through Law or a similar organization.

8. We must subscribe to Christian and conservative publications for an accurate view of what is happening in the world. Remember, nearly every major media outlet in America is controlled or heavily influenced by individuals who are areligious and liberal in their thinking. We are being surfeited with their distorted world view in what we read, see, and hear.

9. Christians must lobby for media review boards in their commu-

nities and states in order to monitor the abuses of the hidden censors of the media. Meet with local church leaders to discuss this idea.

10. We should donate Christian and conservative books to our local libraries. Request that conservative and Christian magazines be made available as well.

11. Join forces with other local churches in your area to produce a weekly television program on the public access cable station in your community. Contact your cable operator for details.

12. Monitor your local TV stations to make certain they are truly serving the public interest. Every TV station must have its license renewed by the FCC every three years. If you feel that your station does not serve the public interest, file a petition to deny renewal of broadcast license. For a solid discussion of this whole process, order the pamphlet "Licensed to Serve," published by the American Legal Foundation, 1612 K Street, N.W., Suite 502, Washington, D.C. 20006.

13. We Christians could use a media clearinghouse of some kind to bring talented writers, directors, and producers together to create Christian films and television programs.

14. We should make every effort to "raise the consciousness" of the American public to the dangerous liberal/humanist biases in our entertainment and news fields, using whatever means are at our disposal to expose the hidden censors of the media.

15. Christians need to get involved in organizations like Don Wildmon's Coalition for Better Television or my wife's organization, Concerned Women for America. We must actively work to change our society.

These are just a few of the ways in which we can challenge the liberal/humanist media establishment in America. Obviously no one person can possibly do all of the things listed. But if you can act on some of these suggestions and implement them, you will be making a significant contribution to the cause of Christ and personal freedom in America.

We must have a free press and wholesome family entertainment. Neither exists right now. And whether we *will* enjoy these in the future depends, in large measure, on your prayers and actions. So get busy *praying and working.*

Appendix A
Conservative/Christian Organizations and Publications

While I do not necessarily personally endorse the purposes of these organizations or agree with everything they publish, I am listing them for your use. The hidden censors of the media have a monopoly on the *major* means of communication: television, film, and large-circulation magazines. *But there are alternate sources of reliable information for us to use in making intelligent decisions about the world around us.*

Instead of receiving information that has been filtered through the minds of liberals or humanists, we should wisely utilize resources of organizations and publications that espouse a Christian conservative viewpoint. Once you begin reading some of these publications, you will discover a whole different world out there than the one presented in *Time* magazine or on the "NBC Nightly News." You would do well to subscribe to several of the magazines and newspapers listed and get involved in one or more of the organizations described.

American Opinion, 395 Concord Avenue, Belmont, MA 02178. A monthly journal of conservative political opinion. Twenty-five dollars a year.

Baptists for Life, 2113 Alamo National Building, San Antonio, TX 78205. A prolife group.

Bob Larson Ministries, Box 36480, Denver, CO 80236. Bob Larson publishes books, pamphlets, and cassettes on issues facing contemporary Christians: drug abuse, sexual immorality, humanism, pornography. Order free catalog.

Censored, a publication listing over 750 organizations and publications ranging from far left to far right. Excellent resource material. Eight dollars a copy. Order from: B. Corbett, P.O. Box 1526, Bonita Springs, FL 33923.

Chalcedon Report, P.O. Box 158, Vallecito, CA 95251. Monthly publication of Dr. Rousas J. Rushdoony. Primary interest is religious freedom and battle against humanism.

Christian Family Renewal, P.O. Box 73, Clovis, CA 93613. Concerned with moral issues facing Christian families. Write for catalog.

Christian Research, 279 Spring Street, Eureka Springs, AK 72632.

Citizens for Decency Through Law, 2331 West Royal Palm Road #105, Phoenix, AZ 85107. One of the largest and most effective anti-pornography groups in America.

Concerned Women for American Education & Legal Defense Foundation. P.O. Box 5100, San Diego, CA 92105. I can recommend this organization without hesitation, because my wife founded it. CWA is a membership organization of women who gather to pray about issues of concern to Christians. Membership is ten dollars a year.

Conservative Book Club, 15 Oakland Avenue, Harrison, NY 10528.

Conservative Digest, 7777 Leesburg Pike, Falls Church, VA 22043. This conservative magazine is published monthly. Eighteen dollars a year.

Editorial Research Service, P.O. Box 1832, Kansas City, MO 64141. Publishes Directory of the American Right, $12.95; Directory of the American Left, $12.95; Bibliography of the American Right, $9.95; Bibliography of the American Left, $9.95.

The Foundation for Christian Self-Government, P.O. Box 1087, Thousand Oaks, CA 91360. A conservative, Christian organization working to restore America's Christian heritage. Leadership training workshops, publications available. Write for details.

The Heritage Foundation, 913 C Street, N.E., Washington, D.C. 20002. A conservative think tank. Write for a catalog of publications.

Human Events, 422 First Street, S.E., Washington, D.C. 20003. Excellent weekly newspaper. Six-month subscription, $13.00; full year, $25.00.

The Moral Majority Report, 499 South Capitol Street, Washington, D.C. 20003. Fifteen dollars a year.

The Barbara M. Morris Report, P.O. Box 756, Upland, CA 91786. Barbara Morris focuses upon humanism in the public schools. Write for more information.

National Christian Action Coalition, P.O. Box 1745, Washington, D.C. 20013

NFD Informer, National Federation for Decency, Box 1398, Tupelo, MS 38801. Ten dollars a year. This publication is written by the Reverend Donald Wildmon. Keeps NFD members up to date on current battle against the major television networks.

The Review of the News, 395 Concord Avenue, Belmont, MA 02178. High-quality weekly conservative news magazine. Twenty-five dollars a year.

The Phyllis Schlafly Report, Box 618, Alton, IL 62002. Ten dollars a year. Phyllis Schlafly will keep you informed on current anti-ERA activities. Highly recommended.

Appendix B
Media Watchdog
Organizations

National News Council
1 Lincoln Plaza
New York, NY   10023

National Citizens Committee for Broadcasting
1028 Connecticut Avenue NW
Washington, D.C.   20004

Federal Communications Commission
1919 M Street, NW
Washington, D.C.   20554

National Association for Better Broadcasting
2615 Westwood Blvd.
Los Angeles, CA

Accuracy in Media
1341 G Street, NW
Washington, D.C.   20005
(Reed Irvine, founder of AIM, publishes excellent four-page *AIM Report,* twice a month. Subscription: Fifteen dollars mailed third class; thirty dollars mailed first class)

For a free list of media personalities who are now or who have been members of the Council on Foreign Relations or the Trilateral Commission, send a stamped, self-addressed envelope to:
Family Seminars
P.O. Box 16000
San Diego, CA 92116

Source Notes

Chapter 1

1. *Religious Broadcasting,* (January 1982), p. 21.
2. Ibid., p. 22
3. "*Time* Poll Says 60% Think TV 'Bad for the Country,' " *NFD Informer* (July 1981).
4. "Peeping Tom Reality," *The Capsule* (May/June 1982), p. 7.
5. Ibid.
6. Ibid.
7. "Noted Author Writes Concerning Secular Humanism and the Media," *NFD Informer* (November 1982), p. 6.
8. Ibid.
9. Ibid.
10. Geoffrey Wolff, "Shortcuts to the Heart," *Esquire* (August 1981), p. 48.
11. "Profile," *The Review of the News* (17 March 1982), p. 63.
12. Ibid.
13. "Noted Author," p. 8.
14. Donald Wildmon, "A Time for Decision," *Religious Broadcasting* (April 1982), p. 24.
15. "TV Suicide Reports and Copycats Linked," *San Diego Union* (11 January 1983), p. D-1.
16. Ted Turner in a *Penthouse* magazine interview.
17. Eugene H. Methvin, "TV Violence: The Shocking New Evidence," *Reader's Digest* (January 1983), p. 49.
18. Thomas Radecki, "How Violent Is Television?" *Christian Herald* (September 1982), p. 58.
19. Ibid.
20. Methvin, p. 50.
21. Ibid., p. 51.
22. Bonnie Remsberg, "Jeremy's Tragedy," *Family Circle* (5 October 1982), p. 158.
23. Ibid., p. 40.
24. Ron Powers, "The New 'Holy War' Against Sex and Violence," *TV Guide* (18 April 1981), p. 8.

25. Ibid.
26. "Noted Author," p. 6.
27. George Orwell, *1984* (New York: Signet Classic, 1962), pp. 205, 206.

Chapter 2

1. "A Look at the Media Elite," *The Capsule* (May/June 1982), p. 4.
2. Ibid.
3. "Poll Finds Americans Skeptical of News Media," *Washington Post* (27 April 1981).
4. Alvin P. Sanoff, "The Press: In Deeper Trouble With Public," *U.S. News & World Report* (20 September 1982), p. 68.
5. Ibid.
6. Ibid.
7. Ibid.
8. Ibid.
9. Ibid.
10. "Nobel Laureate Criticizes the Western Press," *Forum Bulletin* 1:5.
11. Franky Schaeffer, *A Time for Anger* (Westchester, Ill.: Good News, 1981), p. 39.
12. Michael J. O'Neill, speech given to the American Society of Newspaper Editors, May 5, 1982.
13. M. Lyle Spencer, *Editorial Writing: Ethics, Policy, Practice* (Boston: Houghton Mifflin, 1924), p. 25.
14. Ibid., p. 23.
15. Curtis D. MacDougall, *Interpretative Reporting* (New York: Macmillan, 1963), p. 14.
16. Ibid., p. 17.
17. Richard F. Pourade, "New Disturbing Journalistic Era Opens," *Human Events* (13 October 1961), p. 673.
18. Francis X. Gannon, *A Biographical Dictionary of the Left*, 4 vols. (Belmont, Mass.: Western Islands, 1969–1971), 2:484.
19. S. Robert Lichter and Stanley Rothman, "Media & Business Elites," *Public Opinion* (October/November 1981), p. 42.
20. Ibid., p. 43.
21. Ibid.
22. Ibid., p. 44.
23. Ibid., p. 45.
24. Ibid.
25. Ibid., p. 60, *italics mine.*
26. Ibid.
27. *The Connecticut Mutual Life Report on American Values in the 80s: The Impact of Belief*, 1981, p. 2.

28. Ibid., p. 6.
29. Ibid., p. 28.
30. Ibid., p. 31.

Chapter 3

1. Barry Goldwater, *The Conscience of a Majority* (New York: Pocket Books, 1971), pp. 149, 150.
2. Ibid., p. 151.
3. Francis X. Gannon, *A Biographical Dictionary of the Left,* 4 vols. (Belmont, Mass.: Western Islands, 1969–1973), 2:273, 274.
4. Edith Efron, "There *Is* A Network News Bias," *TV Guide* (28 February 1970), p. 11.
5. Ibid.
6. John Rees, "Infiltration of the Media by the KGB and Its Friends" *Accuracy in Media* (1978), pp. 3, 4.
7. Ibid., p. 4.
8. James L. Tyson, *Target America: The Influence of Communist Propaganda on U.S. Media* (Chicago: Regnery Gateway, 1981), p. 9.
9. Rees, pp. 27, 28.
10. Rees, p. 6.
11. Rees, p. 18.
12. Walter Duranty, *I Write As I Please* (New York: Simon & Schuster, 1935), p. 340.
13. Malcolm Muggeridge, *Chronicles of a Wasted Time: The Green Stick* (New York: William Morrow, 1973) pp. 255, 256.
14. "Testimony of Juanita Castro Ruz," *Committee on Un-American Activities* (11 June 1965), p. 848.
15. W. Cleon Skousen, *The Naked Communist* (Salt Lake City: Ensign, 1962), pp. 240, 241.
16. Ibid., p. 240.
17. "The Ray Bonner Division," *AIM Report* (July 1982), 2:1, 2.
18. Ibid., p. 2.
19. Ibid., p. 1.
20. *AIM Report* (March 1982), p. 4.
21. Philip Taubman, "Salvadorans' U.S. Campaign: Selling of Revolution," *New York Times* (26 February 1982), p. A-10.
22. *AIM Report* (April 1982), 1:1.
23. Benjamin Gitlow, *The Whole of Their Lives* (Belmont, Mass.: Western Islands, 1965), p. 72.
24. Ibid., p. 70.
25. Ibid., p. 69.
26. Ibid., p. 81.

27. W. Cleon Skousen, *The Naked Capitalist* (Salt Lake City: Reviewer, 1970), p. 1.
28. Ibid., pp. 20, 21.
29. Carroll Quigley, *Tragedy and Hope* (New York: Macmillan Company, 1966), p. 950.
30. Ibid., p. 953.
31. Ibid., p. 956.
32. Ibid., p. 950.
33. Chester Ward and Phyllis Schlafly, *Kissinger on the Couch* (New Rochelle, N.Y.: Arlington House Publishers, 1975), p. 146.
34. *Humanist Manifestos I and II* (Buffalo, N.Y.: Prometheus Books, 1973), p. 21.
35. Richard Gardner, "The Hard Road to World Order," *Foreign Affairs* (April 1974), p. 558.
36. William E. Dunham, "Beware the Council on Foreign Relations," *The Review of the News* (9 February 1977), p. 2.
37. Zbigniew Brzezinski, *Between Two Ages: America's Role in the Technetronic Era* (New York: Penguin Books, 1970), pp. 296, 297.

Chapter 4

1. E. Foster Marshall and Mary E. Swanson, *The American Covenant* (Thousand Oaks, Calif.: Foundation for Christian Self-Government, 1981), p. 16.
2. Clarence Manion, *The Key to Peace* (Washington, D.C.: Heritage Foundation, 1951), p. 46.
3. Francis A. Schaeffer, *A Christian Manifesto* (Westchester, Ill.: Good News, 1981), p. 46.
4. *Humanist Manifestos I and II* (Buffalo, N.Y.: Prometheus Books, 1973), p. 13.
5. Dr. Rousas J. Rushdoony, "Injustice in the Name of Justice," *Chalcedon Report* (January 1983).
6. *Humanist Manifestos,* p. 18.
7. Ibid., p. 21.
8. Foster and Swanson, p. 16.
9. Franky Schaeffer, *A Time for Anger* (Westchester, Ill.: Good News, 1981), author's foreword.
10. Dr. Rousas J. Rushdoony, *Chalcedon Report* (December 1981).

Chapter 5

1. John Fulton Lewis, "Who Are Those Guys?" *The Media Institute,* p. 1.

2. Reader's Digest Editors, eds., *The Story of America* (New York: Random House, 1975), p. 356.
3. Ibid.
4. Ibid., p. 358.
5. Frank Luther Mott, *American Journalism* (New York: Macmillan, 1962), p. 243.
6. Ibid., p. 527.
7. Ibid., p. 529.
8. John C. Merrill, *The Elite Press* (Marshfield, Mass.: Pitman Publishing, 1968), p. 3.
9. Ibid., p. 11.
10. James Reston, *The Artillery of the Press* (New York: Harper & Row, 1967), p. vii.
11. Leonard Silk and Mark Silk, *The American Establishment* (New York: Basic Books, 1980), p. 68.
12. W. Cleon Skousen, *The Naked Capitalist* (Salt Lake City: Reviewer, 1970), p. 34.
13. "New, Disturbing Journalistic Era Opens," *Human Events* (13 October 1961), p. 673.
14. Ibid.
15. Ibid.
16. Ibid., p. 674.
17. "Writers' Wronger," *AIM Report* (April 1983), p. 4.
18. Ibid.
19. Wendell Rawls, Jr., "UPI Ownership Transfers Seem to Involve Little Cash," *New York Times* (9 February 1983), p. B-13.
20. Barry Goldwater, *The Conscience of the Majority* (New York: Pocket Books, 1971), p. 178.
21. Ibid., p. 179.
22. Victor Lasky, *It Didn't Start With Watergate* (New York: Dial Press, 1977), p. 1.
23. "Most Admired Men Poll," *Good Housekeeping* (January 1983).
24. Stephen Strang, "The Power Within," *Charisma* (January 1983), p. 29.
25. "Watt Lauds His Tenure, Assails Media for Distortion," *San Diego Union* (8 February 1983), p. A-3.
26. Ibid.
27. Ibid.
28. Strang, p. 26.
29. Goldwater, p. 155.

Chapter 6

1. General William Westmoreland, in a letter sent to potential subscribers of the Accuracy in Media organization's *AIM Report* (March 1983).

2. Don Kowet and Sally Bedell, "Anatomy of a Smear: How CBS News Broke the Rules and 'Got' Gen. Westmoreland," *TV Guide* (29 May 1983), p. 2.
3. Suzanne Choney, "Journalists Urged to Enforce Ethics," *San Diego Union* (14 November 1982), p. A-20.
4. David Shaw, "Press Takes Inward Look at Its Ethics," *Los Angeles Times* (23 September 1981), p. 24.
5. Ibid., p. 25.
6. Ibid., p. 26.
7. Michael J. O'Neill in a speech given to the American Society of Newspaper Editors in May 1982.
8. Dan Neuharth, "Beatty, Redford on Media: 'No Privacy.'" *USA Today* (11 May 1983).

Chapter 7

1. Joseph Keeley, *The Left-Leaning Antenna: Political Bias in Television* (New Rochelle, N.Y.: Crown Pubs., 1971), p. 206.
2. Sydney W. Head, *Broadcasting in America* (Boston, Mass.: Houghton Mifflin, 1956), p. 93.
3. Ibid., p. 92.
4. Ibid., p. 112.
5. Ibid.
6. *The National Cyclopaedia of American Biography,* Vol. A (Clifton, N.J.: James T. White Company, 1930), p. 81.
7. Ibid., p. 82.
8. Carroll Quigley, *Tragedy and Hope: A History of the World in Our Times* (New York: Macmillan, 1966), p. 952.
9. Head, et al., p. 113.
10. Gary Allen and Larry Abraham, *None Dare Call It Conspiracy* (Seal Beach, Calif.: Concord Press, 1971), p. 89.
11. W. Cleon Skousen, *The Naked Capitalist* (Salt Lake City: Reviewer, 1970), p. 40.
12. Head, et al., p. 121.
13. Ibid., p. 118.
14. Bob Shanks, *The Cool Fire: How to Make It in Television* (New York: Random House, 1977), p. 51.
15. Head, et al., p. 131.
16. William S. Paley, *As It Happened* (Garden City, N.Y.: Doubleday, 1979), p. 35.
17. Ibid., p. 42.
18. Ibid., p. 43.
19. Ibid., p. 106.

20. Ibid., p. 205.
21. Dan Smoot, *The Invisible Government* (Dallas, Tex.: Dan Smoot Report, 1962), p. 124.
22. Paley, pp. 338, 339.
23. Head, et al., p. 141.
24. *Who Was Who in America,* Vol. 3, 1951–1960 (Chicago: Marquis) p. 641.
25. Gary Allen, "The Media," *American Opinion* (September 1970), p. 13.
26. Shanks, p. 67.
27. Everett C. Parker, "Communities Versus the TV Networks" *New York Times* (25 September 1977), p. D-27.
28. A. Frank Reel, *The Networks: How They Stole the Show* (New York: Scribner's, 1979), p. x.
29. Ibid., p. 44.
30. Les Brown, *Keeping Your Eye on Television* (New York: Pilgrim Press, 1979), p. 53.
31. Shanks, p. 99.
32. Ibid., p. 245.
33. Paley, p. 264.
34. Reel, p. 8.
35. Tony Schwartz, *Media: The Second God* (New York: Random House, 1982), pp. 4, 5.
36. Brown, p. 20.
37. Reel, p. 15.
38. "Networks Missing Another 1.5 Million Viewers," *State Times* (Baton Rouge, La.), (9 December 1982).
39. "Where Did All the Viewers Go?" *San Diego Union* (29 October 1982), p. C-13.
40. "Networks Missing."
41. "Where Did All?" p. C-13.
42. James Mann, "Networks' Heyday in TV Coming to a Close?" *U.S. News & World Report* (5 April 1982), p. 62.
43. Richard Corliss, "Troubled Times for the Networks," *Time* (7 February 1983), p. 78.

Chapter 8

1. Dotson Rader, "Bette," *Parade* (6 March 1983), p. 6.
2. Ibid.
3. Arthur Knight, *The Liveliest Art,* rev. ed. (New York: New American Library, 1979), p. 113.
4. Eric Rhode, *A History of the Cinema From Its Origins to 1970* (New York: Hill & Wang, 1976), p. 335.
5. Ibid., p. 336.

6. Philip French, *The Movie Moguls* (Chicago: Contemporary Books, 1969), p. 17.
7. Sydney W. Head, et al., *Broadcasting in America* (Boston: Houghton Mifflin, 1956), pp. 455–464.
8. French, p. 85.
9. "Movie Trend Continues to Display Total Nudity," *College Times* (California State), (26 January 1971).
10. "To Scorsese 'Comedy' Is Not Funny," *Los Angeles Times* (15 March 1983), 6:5.
11. Ibid.
12. " 'Bad Boys' Producer Offers No Apologies," *Los Angeles Times* (2 April 1983), 6:1.
13. Frank Capra, *Frank Capra: The Name Above the Title* (New York: Macmillan, 1971), p. 468.
14. Ibid., p. 493.
15. W. Cleon Skousen, *The Naked Capitalist* (Salt Lake City: Reviewer, 1970), p. 34.
16. Robert Sklar, *Movie-Made America: A Cultural History of American Movies* (New York: Random House, 1975), p. 146.
17. Rhode, p. 262.
18. Sklar, p. 162.
19. Rhode, p. 264.
20. Sklar, p. 289.
21. Rhode, p. 83.
22. Larry Ceplair and Steven Englund, *The Inquisition in Hollywood: Politics in the Film Community 1930–1960* (Garden City, N.Y.: Doubleday, 1980), p. 256.
23. Ibid., p. 66.
24. French, p. 149.
25. Ibid., p. 124.
26. Donald Spoto, *Stanley Kramer: Film Maker* (New York: Putnam, 1978), pp. 327–344.
27. "A Blacklist in Hollywood? Ask Lester Cole," *San Diego Union* (12 January 1982), p. D-1.
28. John Benedict, "Movies Are Redder Than Ever," *American Mercury* (August 1960), p. 16.
29. Spoto, pp. 327–344.
30. "Dealing in Stardom: Drugs Pervade Hollywood," *Santa Ana Register* (31 October 1982), p. A-17.
31. Ibid.
32. Ibid.
33. Ben Stein, *The View From Sunset Boulevard* (New York: Doubleday, 1980), p. xiii.
34. Ibid.

35. Ibid., pp. 3, 4.
36. Ibid., p. 13.
37. Ibid., p. 20.
38. Ibid.
39. Ibid., p. 19.
40. Ibid., p. 24.
41. Ibid., pp. 29, 30.
42. Ibid., p. 33.
43. Ibid.
44. Ibid., p. 54.
45. Ibid., p. 62.
46. Ibid., p. 102.
47. Franky Schaeffer, *A Time for Anger* (Westchester, Ill.: Good News, 1981), p. 28.
48. Stein, p. 136.
49. Lichter, Lichter, and Rothman, "Hollywood and America: The Odd Couple," *Public Opinion* (December/January 1983), p. 55.
50. Ibid.
51. Ibid.
52. Ibid.
53. Ibid., p. 56.
54. Ibid., p. 57.
55. Ibid.
56. Ibid., p. 58.

Chapter 9

1. Margaret O'Brien Steinfels and Peter Steinfels, "The New Awakening: Getting Religion in the Video Age," *Channels of Communication* (January/February 1983), p. 24.
2. Ibid.
3. Howard Jones, "The Urgency of Broadcasting," *Religious Broadcasting* (February 1981), p. 36.
4. Jerry Falwell, "Church and Media: The Vital Partnership," *Religious Broadcasting* (February 1981), p. 56.
5. Tom Bissett, "Religious Broadcasting Comes of Age," *Christianity Today* (4 September 1981), p. 33.
6. Ibid., p. 34.
7. Jamie Buckingham, "Still Shouting It From the Housetops," *Charisma* (April 1983), p. 21.
8. Ibid., p. 20.
9. *Together* (January-February 1983), p. 8.
10. *The Miracle Birth of Trinity Broadcasting Network,* pp. 5–9.

11. Michael Hernandez, "Five Issues: A Critical Report on Christian Broadcasting," *Focus* (Summer 1979), pp. 9, 10.
12. Falwell, p. 57.
13. Dan Wooding, "Buzz," (unpublished manuscript).
14. Ibid.
15. Jimmy Swaggart, "Clean Up Our Act," *Charisma* (November 1982), p. 25.
16. Bissett, p. 35.

Chapter 10

1. Gerhard J. Hanneman and William J. McEwen, *Communication and Behavior* (Reading, Mass.: Addison-Wesley, 1975), p. 335.
2. Ibid.
3. Les Brown, "Cable's Marauders," *Channels of Communication* (February 1983), p. 12.
4. Laura Landro, "Cable-TV Bidding War to Serve Large Cities Is Quickly Cooling Off," *Wall Street Journal* (1 April 1983), p. 1.
5. Ibid.
6. Ibid.
7. "Court Ruling May Cut Cable TV Viewing," *Los Angeles Times* (14 March 1983), p. 12.
8. "Public Access TV in New York Tends Toward Sex, Sadism," *Wall Street Journal* (20 December 1982), p. 1.
9. Ibid., p. 14.
10. Ibid.
11. Frank York, "Pulling the Plug on Pornography," *Charisma* (January 1983), p. 46.
12. Ibid.
13. Ibid., p. 47.
14. Ibid.
15. Ibid.
16. Ibid.

Chapter 11

1. A. Frank Reel, *The Networks: How They Stole the Show* (New York: Charles Scribner's Sons, 1979), p. 135.
2. Rob Greene, "Should We Have Live Suicides on TV?" *San Diego Union* (1 November 1982), p. B-11.

Bibliography

Allen, Gary, and Abraham, Larry. *None Dare Call It Conspiracy*. Seal Beach, Calif.: Concord Press, 1971.

Brown, Les. *Keeping Your Eye on Television*. New York: Pilgrim Press, 1979.

Capra, Frank. *The Name Above the Title*. New York: Macmillan, 1971.

Ceplair, Larry, and Englund, Steven. *The Inquisition in Hollywood: Politics in the Film Community 1930–1960*. Garden City, N.Y.: Doubleday, 1980.

Foster, Marshall E., and Swanson, Mary E. *The American Covenant: The Untold Story*. Thousand Oaks, Calif.: Foundation for Christian Self-Government, 1981.

French, Philip. *The Movie Moguls*. Chicago: Contemporary Books, 1969.

Gannon, Francis X. *A Biographical Dictionary of the Left*, Vol. 1. Belmont, Mass.: Western Islands, 1969.

——— *A Biographical Dictionary of the Left*, Vol. 2. Belmont, Mass.: Western Islands, 1971.

——— *A Biographical Dictionary of the Left*, Vol. 4. Belmont, Mass.: Western Islands, 1973.

Gitlow, Benjamin. *The Whole of Their Lives*. Belmont, Mass.: Western Islands, 1965.

Goldwater, Barry. *The Conscience of a Majority*. New York: Pocket Books, 1971.

Hanneman, Gerhard J., and McEwen, William J. *Communication and Behavior*. Reading, Mass.: Addison-Wesley, 1975.

Head, Sydney W. et al. *Broadcasting in America*. Boston: Houghton Mifflin, 1956.

Humanist Manifestos I and II. Buffalo, N.Y.: Prometheus Books, 1973.

Keeley, Joseph. *The Left-Leaning Antenna: Political Bias in Television*. New Rochelle, N.Y.: Crown Pubs., 1971.

Knight, Arthur. *The Liveliest Art*. Rev. ed. New York: New American Library, 1979.

MacDougall, Curtis D. *Interpretative Reporting*. New York: MacMillan, 1963.

Manion, Clarence. *The Key to Peace*. Washington, D.C.: Heritage Foundation, 1951.

Merrill, John C. *The Elite Press*. Marshfield, Mass.: Pitman Publishing, 1968.

Mott, Frank Luther. *American Journalism*. New York: Macmillan, 1962.

The National Cyclopedia of American Biography. Vol. A. Clifton, N.J.: James T. White, 1930.

Orwell, George. *1984*. New York: Signet Classics, 1962.

Paley, William S. *As It Happened*. Garden City, N.Y.: Doubleday, 1979.

Quigley, Carroll. *Tragedy and Hope: A History of the World in Our Times*. New York: Macmillan, 1966.

Reader's Digest Editors, eds. *The Story of America*. New York: Random House, 1975.

Reel, A. Frank. *The Networks: How They Stole the Show*. New York: Scribner, 1979.

Reston, James. *The Artillery of the Press*. New York: Harper & Row, 1967.

Rhode, Eric. *A History of the Cinema From Its Origins to 1970*. New York: Hill & Wang, 1976.

Schaeffer, Francis A. *A Christian Manifesto*. Westchester, Ill.: Good News, 1981.

Schaeffer, Franky. *A Time for Anger*. Westchester, Ill.: Good News, 1981.

Schwartz, Tony. *Media: The Second God*. New York: Random House, 1982.

Shanks, Bob. *The Cool Fire: How to Make It in Television*. New York: Random House, 1977.

Silk, Leonard, and Silk, Mark. *The American Establishment*. New York: Basic Books, 1980.

Sklar, Robert. *Movie-Made America: A Cultural History of American Movies*. New York: Random House, 1976.

Skousen, W. Cleon. *The Naked Communist*. Salt Lake City: Ensign, 1962.

————— *The Naked Capitalist*. Salt Lake City: Reviewer, 1970.

Smoot, Dan. *The Invisible Government*. Dallas, Tex.: Dan Smoot Report, 1962.

Spencer, M. Lyle. *Editorial Writing: Ethics, Policy, Practice*. Boston: Houghton Mifflin, 1924.

Spoto, Donald. *Stanley Kramer: Film Maker*. New York: Putnam, 1978.

Stein, Ben. *The View From Sunset Boulevard*. New York: Doubleday, 1980.

Talese, Gay. *The Kingdom and the Power*. New York: Dell, 1981.

Tyson, James L. *Target America: The Influence of Communist Propaganda on U.S. Media*. Chicago: Regnery Gateway, 1981.

Who Was Who in America. Chicago: Marquis, Vol. 3, 1951–1960.

About the Author

TIM LAHAYE is a well-known evangelical spokesman, Christian educator, and outspoken advocate of family life and pro-moral concerns. He earned his Doctor of Ministry degree from Western Conservative Baptist Seminary and served as a pastor for thirty years. He is founder of Family Life Seminars, which he and his wife, Beverly, conduct throughout the United States and Canada. Tim and Beverly also minister to thousands through their nationally aired television program, "The LaHayes on Family Life." Dr. LaHaye's many best-selling books include *How to Be Happy Though Married, Understanding the Male Temperament, The Battle for the Mind, The Battle for the Family,* and *The Battle for the Public Schools;* and *Spirit-Controlled Family Living* and *The Act of Marriage,* co-written with Beverly.